Praise for
Every Young Woman's Battle

"*Every Young Woman's Battle* is shockingly honest and straightforward, which is exactly what this generation needs. I think Shannon Ethridge takes the perfect approach in dealing with some sensitive topics. The result is a very true, honest, and effective look at issues facing young women today."

> —SARAH KELLY, recording artist for Gotee Records

"Like a steady IV drip, today's teenage girls get a message of confused and cheapened sexuality. They are desperate for reasons to guard and preserve themselves. Shannon Ethridge gives girls reasons in this relevant and readable book. Every young woman and every young woman's mother need to read this book!"

> —SHARON HERSH, author of *"Mom, I Feel Fat!"* and *"Mom, I Hate My Life!"*

"I'm so grateful that Shannon decided to be as honest and real as she is—that's the only way this book could be as powerful as it is…. God is going to heal in unbelievable ways through this potent work of art and heart!… I can honestly say that this book has changed me—because it gives a clear picture of who Jesus is, who we are as His bride, and why we can't seem to be satisfied with anything or anyone else."

> —BETHANY DILLON, songwriter and recording artist

"A must-read for every teenage girl! Honest and informative, this book is not only highly readable with its true-to-life illustrations, but it's packed with answers for every sexual situation today's teens encounter. What a great antidote for the twisted sexual messages our pop culture continues to dish out. Way to go, Shannon!"

> —MELODY CARLSON, author of Diary of a Teenage Girl series and *Torch Red, Color Me Torn*

"Shannon writes with a forthright style, yet she remains tactful and kind as she presents her balanced, godly teaching on dating and relationships. Without question, this is a must-read for any young woman who longs to remain pure in her relationship with God, and I suspect this book will very quickly become a staple of small-group studies."

—FRED STOEKER, coauthor of *Every Young Man's Battle*

"This book should be required reading for any teenage girl who has been exposed to the negative influences of the culture through media, music, movies, and fashion magazines. As someone who is in the trenches of ministry to teen girls, I appreciate Shannon's candid approach and her willingness to tackle some difficult topics facing our young women. She does a beautiful job of exposing the godless issues of the culture while at the same time offering godly solutions."

—VICKI COURTNEY, founder of Virtuous Reality Ministries and author
of *Your Girl: Raising a Godly Daughter in an Ungodly World*

"This book is awesome! I will be buying it and reading it with teens that I mentor. I wish it had been available to me when I was a teen."

—ADRIENNE FREAS, homemaker and Campus Crusade for Christ staff member

"All I can say is, 'Wow!' Shannon and Steve have done an awesome job. I see excellence and God's wisdom on each page of *Every Young Woman's Battle*. Its practical applications and insights will touch and heal many."

—LISA BEVERE, speaker, cofounder of Messenger International,
and author of *Kissed the Girls and Made Them Cry*

Shannon Ethridge
& Stephen Arterburn

every young woman's battle

Guarding Your Mind, Heart, and Body

in a Sex-Saturated World

WATERBROOK
PRESS

EVERY YOUNG WOMAN'S BATTLE
PUBLISHED BY WATERBROOK PRESS
2375 Telstar Drive, Suite 160
Colorado Springs, Colorado 80920
A division of Random House, Inc.

Names and facts from stories contained in this book have been changed, but the emotional and sexual struggles portrayed are true stories as related to the authors through personal interviews, letters, or e-mails.

ISBN 1-57856-856-0

Published in association with the literary agency of Alive Communications, Inc., 7680 Goddard Street, Suite 200, Colorado Springs, CO 80920.

Library of Congress Cataloging-in-Publication Data

Ethridge, Shannon.
    Every young woman's battle / Shannon Ethridge and Stephen Arterburn.
       p. cm.
    Includes bibliographical references.
    ISBN 1-57856-856-0
    1. Young women—Religious life.   2. Young women—Conduct of life.   I. Arterburn, Stephen, 1953– II. Title.
    BV4551.3.E84 2004
    241'.66—dc22

                                               2004002068

Printed in the United States of America
2005

10 9 8 7 6

contents

Have you ever become frustrated working through a maze in a puzzle book? The goal is to discover a pathway from the starting point to the end without crossing over any lines. However, the multitude of dead ends can make this a true test of your patience and concentration.

Imagine a *giant* maze the size of a football field. Suppose someone offers you a ten-thousand-dollar reward if you can successfully make your way from start to finish within four minutes. You are certainly motivated, but when you enter the maze, you find that you can't see anything but the nine-foot-high walls directly in front and on each side of you. There are no markers to direct your path, and you have no way of discerning when a dead end is right around the corner. Your chances of victory are next to impossible. You need the help of a trusted advisor who is more familiar with this maze than you are.

If my daughter asked me to help her with such a challenge, do you know what I would do? I'd get a forty-foot ladder and two cell phones. I'd give one phone to her and carry the other with me to the top of the ladder where I'd have an aerial view of the maze. Then I'd call her to give guidance from above. I could warn her when she follows a dead end path, and I would tell her when to turn right and when to turn left.

Now let me ask you this: Would my daughter choose to disregard my instructions and attempt to trust her own sense of direction in that giant maze? Of course not. She would listen carefully to my every word, because she knows that I can see things ahead that she can't, that I am worthy of her trust, and that I love her and want her to succeed.

All young people face a similar challenge, only the prize is much greater than a measly ten thousand dollars. The prize is the health, happiness, peace, and contentment that come from saving yourself for marriage, choosing a good mate, and bringing beautiful children into the world. I have four such children, and after thirty years of being a husband and a dad, I can honestly tell you that nothing on this side of heaven brings me greater joy than my family. You're probably one of the 93 percent of teenagers who expect to marry someday and the 91 percent who hope to have children.[1] If so, please know that your entire future, including your ability to have a successful marriage and your own children someday, is made up of one decision after another. You may not always have the foresight to know where each decision will lead you.

Proverbs 14:12 says, "There is a way that seems right to a man, but in the end it leads to death." All over the world, young people are making wrong decisions that seem right to them. Whether it's the movies they watch or the lies they tell their parents or how far they're willing to go on a date, many young people think, *It's no big deal… Everybody does it… It feels right to me.* They can't tell the difference between right and wrong, because they have no moral compass to direct them in the path of absolute truth.

Because of their poor sense of direction, many of your peers are making decisions that lead them not toward an abundant, joy-filled life, but toward destruction and even death. Each day in the United States,

- 4,219 teenagers contract a sexually transmitted disease, and many of these will later face a premature death as a result;
- 1,106 teenage girls abort their unborn babies; and
- 6 teens commit suicide, often because of a broken heart or out of guilt over a premarital sexual relationship.[2]

Every single day we lose precious lives because of one former decision made in the heat of the moment. Choices that seem right to these young people eventually lead down the wrong path entirely.

You have to decide whether you are going to trust your own judgment in your pursuit of sexual purity or whether you are going to look to a trusted advisor for guidance. Even though I can't be waiting on a forty-foot ladder for your cell phone call, I want you to know that you have a heavenly Father who sees the big picture, knows exactly which turns lead to dead ends, and recognizes the clear path toward victory. God has divine knowledge of where each and every decision will take you.

Isaiah 30:21 says, "Whether you turn to the right or to the left, your ears will hear a voice behind you, saying, 'This is the way; walk in it.' " You may not hear an audible voice with the ears on your head, but if you are trusting in Jesus Christ to guide you through life's maze, you can hear Him with the ears of your heart—if you tune out the distractions of the world and listen for His perfect direction. He will not fail you in your time of need. He is completely trustworthy. He loves you so much, and He certainly wants to see you succeed.

As a matter of fact, He so desires that you consistently choose the right path that He gave you a road map (the Bible) and a trusted advisor (the Holy Spirit) to guide you. You may think that God is some kind of cosmic kill-joy who just throws out a bunch of "thou shalt nots" to steal all your fun. But God's commandments offer us valuable precepts—or guidelines—to live by. These precepts will do two things: protect you and provide for you. Think of these precepts as an umbrella. As long as you walk under them, you are protected from getting wet and provided with dryness and comfort. But moving out from underneath that umbrella brings uncomfortable consequences. Similarly, when you cherish your sexuality and guard it according to God's plan, you'll be protected from sexually transmitted diseases, unplanned pregnancy, unhealthy relationships, and extreme emotional roller-coaster rides. You'll be provided with safety and security and hope for a promising future. If, however, you ignore God's guidance and move out from under His precepts, you will most certainly experience painful consequences down the road.

Over the past four decades, I've spoken to over seven million young people in over eighty-four countries about *Why True Love Waits,* how to discern *Right from Wrong,* and most recently how to move *Beyond Belief to Convictions.* Most of the questions I receive from teenagers as I travel and speak have to do with sex, love, or dating relationships. While I'm concerned about what you and your peers may be tempted to do when alone with the opposite sex, I'm more concerned with what you believe about your sexuality and God's desire for your purity. That's why I'm thrilled that you are holding this book in your hands. I know that you are going to discover it to be an invaluable tool that will lead you down the path toward a renewed mind, a strong spirit, a pure heart, a healthy body, and tremendously rewarding relationships with others and with God. I pray that you'll take every word to heart, apply these principles in your daily life, and allow God to lead you toward the rich prize of a truly abundant life.

If you are a parent reading this, I want to encourage you not just to give this book to your daughter but to read through it with her and talk with her about this traditionally taboo but vitally important topic. If you think that your child doesn't want to discuss such an intimate subject with you, please think again. Although she may not beg you to talk about sex with her, nearly seven out of ten teens (69 percent) agree it would be easier for them to postpone sexual activity and avoid teen pregnancy if they were able to have more open, honest conversations about these topics with their parents. The same percentage also says that they *are* ready to listen to things that parents thought they were *not* ready to hear. When asked about the reasons teenage girls have babies, 78 percent of white and 70 percent of African American teenagers reported lack of communication between a girl and her parents as one of the key factors. Thirty-one percent of teens say that their parents, not their friends, have the most influence on their decisions about sex.[3]

The bottom line is this: When it comes to sexuality, your daughter needs your guidance and wants it probably far more than you realize. Don't wait for her to bring up the topic. That may never happen. Be proactive in helping her develop strong personal convictions about guarding her sexuality and give her a reliable moral compass. Chances are, because of your guidance, love, and trustworthiness, you'll someday watch her emerge as a victor in every young woman's battle for sexual and emotional purity.

—JOSH MCDOWELL

dedication and acknowledgments

from Shannon Ethridge:

For Erin.
You bring unspeakable joy into all of our lives.
I pray your hunger for God and your passion for purity
will only increase as you continue to blossom.

from Stephen Arterburn:

For Madeline.
I am so glad to be your father, and I will always
be there to help you walk in the footsteps
of your heavenly Father.

As always, my first thanks goes to Jesus Christ for entrusting me with the vision for this book. I pray that it's everything You wanted it to be, and that it touches every life You want it to touch.

To Greg, my husband and best friend, thank you for all that you do and all that you are to me and our children. You are a wonderful helpmate and father, and I love you fiercely.

To my "almost as tall as me" baby girl, Erin. Thank you for helping us proof this manuscript to make sure we didn't sound too old-fashioned. You make a delightful writing partner and an even more delightful daughter.

Mister Mattster Monster, you really stepped up to the plate while Mommy was working on this book. I appreciate all of your help around the house and the comic relief that your antics provide. Life would be pretty dull without you.

Thanks to my family and friends who have been so supportive. I appreciate your patience with me and your many prayers that have sustained me.

To my friends at Rockin' C Ranch and others who have made writing retreat places available, thank you for your warm hospitality and for a quiet place to be alone with God and my laptop.

Tracy Kartes, you have been such a blessing to me and to this book. I love you to the moon and back, girlfriend.

To Ron and Katie Luce, Dave Hasz, and the many Honor Academy interns who contributed significantly to this book, a sincere thank you for allowing me to serve alongside you at Teen Mania Ministries. I count it one of my greatest blessings in life.

To Adrienne and Brian Freas, I appreciate how you allowed the Holy Spirit to use you in miraculous ways during the finalizing of this manuscript. You are definitely chosen instruments of God and a true blessing to me and the many girls who'll read this book.

To Don Pape, Laura Barker, and all the folks at WaterBrook Press, thank you so much for colaboring with us to change lives. We make a great team!

To Liz Heaney, my phenomenal editor, thank you for gracing this project with your wisdom and insight. Also, a sincere thanks to all of our "junior editors"—both guys and girls. There are too many of you to name, but you know who you are and so does God. I pray He blesses your socks off for your willingness to contribute.

Last, but certainly not least, a special thank you to Steve Arterburn, Fred Stoeker, Kenny Luck, and Mike Yorkey. It is such an honor and a privilege to partner with you guys. Thank you for laying such a strong foundation with the Every Man series.

—SHANNON ETHRIDGE

a note to parents

In *Every Young Woman's Battle,* we discuss sexual purity from emotional, mental, spiritual, and physical perspectives, teaching readers to guard their minds, hearts, and bodies in this sex-saturated world. We do so using very frank, contemporary language, writing especially for young women in their teens to early twenties.

Perhaps you are wondering how frank we've been or if this book is appropriate for your daughter at this point in her life. If she regularly watches television, listens to pop music, or reads teen magazines, nothing in this book will be too graphic or shocking for her. Our goal is to present a credible, helpful, Christian perspective on the images your daughter is exposed to every day.

If, on the other hand, you believe she is already committed to sexual purity, or you fear that a frank discussion on the topic may be inappropriate for her, we encourage you to review *Every Young Woman's Battle* before passing it on to your daughter. We have made every effort to address sensitive issues with tact and respect, emphasizing God's desire that young women live with sexual integrity. Our commitment to helping young women requires us to be honest and open with them, and we hope that our doing so will pave the way for your daughter to make many healthy choices about her sexuality.

Years ago when I was dating, young men used young women like you for their own pleasure. They manipulated and pressured girls sexually in order to prop up their own flagging egos.

Nothing felt better to these guys than to prove they still "had it," so they would go out and get whatever they wanted from any girl who would give it to them. These young men didn't see girls as people, but as inferior objects there for a guy's pleasure. They judged a young woman by her body parts and how much she exposed them and what she gave away on a date. They never thought much about what she might be feeling or thinking; they just wanted what they wanted, and they expected a girl to give it if she wanted the "relationship" to continue. The way these guys saw it, girls were there to help guys prove they were "real" men.

When I was in high school and college, every young woman had a reputation—those who would "put out" and those who wouldn't. Guys would compare notes—"Did she or didn't she?"—and brag about their sexual conquests. The girls with a reputation for giving guys what they wanted may have gone out on lots of dates, but they didn't have healthy dating relationships. Young men wanted to look, touch, and feel these girls, but they didn't want to commit to a girl with such a reputation. They simply took what they could get for as long as they wanted it, and then moved on to the next sexual target.

The young men of my day would say or do whatever a girl wanted so that she would be willing to give him her body, even if it meant saying things such as "I love you," "You're special," or "I have never felt like this before." He would take her out to eat or to a movie, because he believed those things would ensure that he'd receive payoff at the end of the evening. He'd make her feel loved and cared for because he knew that was how he could get what he wanted from her. But what these young men took, they never gave back. Each time they had sex with a girl, they took a piece of her soul.

Why am I'm telling you this? Because I want you to know what guys are like—even Christian guys. You see, guys haven't changed when it comes to how they view women. The situation has not improved. In fact, in many ways it has become much worse. I don't want you to be used and abused. You are a special creation of God, and He loves you even more than I love my daughter. He wants the best for you, as I want the best for her. God does not want you to be used, nor does He want you to use others. He wants sexual and emotional integrity for you. He has a great life ahead for you, and you can most easily find it if you find a way to live with sexual integrity.

You are growing up in a culture that does not value sexual integrity and purity. Instead, it values instant gratification and pleasure at all costs. Some of you have begun to live by the values of this culture. You have abandoned what you know to be right deep down inside. You have stopped listening to the small voice inside of you that wants to guide you to stay pure and live with self-respect and high self-esteem. Perhaps you no longer resist the sexual advances of young men, or perhaps you have become the aggressor. You may be the one going after the boys and participating in sexual behavior that dishonors God, your family, and yourself. If you have, this book will show you a path to healing and a second chance with God. If you have not, it will help you develop a defense for yourself, your reputation, and the life God intends you to live. My prayer, our prayer, is that you will read this book, believe it, and live according to the truths we present here.

Before you read what my coauthor, Shannon, has written, I want to tell you what has happened to the young men of my day. We have all gotten older, but many have not gotten wiser. Our culture has changed significantly in the past decade. Sadly, the Internet, television, movies, and advertising have made women seem more like objects than ever before. Men have gone from feeding their sexual obsessions with young women to feeding them with sexual images anywhere and everywhere: billboards, lingerie ads, swimsuit special editions, over two million porn sites, and network television shows. They've become hooked on images, counterfeits of the real thing. Everywhere they look they see women as objects of gratification. Believe me—more men than ever are looking at women as objects to be used for their own pleasure. For every man it's a battle just to view women in the proper light. For many it's the battle of a lifetime.

The more a guy sees and experiences pornography and other sexually explicit images, the more he wants. He tells himself he is just being a man, just doing what all men do. "It's normal" or "It's not hurting anyone," he says as his focus shifts more away from the real women in his life and more and more to the unreal world of sexual gratification at any cost. Many husbands—even Christian husbands—regularly enter a private world of sexual pleasure and shame. For many, sex inside of marriage is no longer enough because they have become hooked on sex as conceived by our wayward culture.

Many men want out but have not known how to get out. About three years ago, Fred Stoeker and I wrote a book called *Every Man's Battle* because we wanted to give men a strategy for freedom and help them win this battle. The book quickly became a best seller and remains on the bestseller list today. The fathers who read it wanted something for their sons, so Fred Stoeker and I wrote *Every Young Man's Battle*. It, too, hit the bestseller list. Fred and I began receiving hundreds of e-mails and a few letters from young men saying that the book had changed their perspective on sex and young women and that they wanted to live the life of sexual integrity that we had written about.

Then something else began to happen. We began receiving e-mails from women expressing a desire for a book of their own on sexual integrity. They, too, wanted to live according to God's standard. Additionally, readers of *Every Woman's Battle* asked for a book for their daughters, so Shannon and I decided to write the book you hold in your hands. We hope it meets a tremendous need for frank talk about your sexuality and that it gives you some solid answers on how to live in a culture designed to throw you off God's track.

You have a job to do, one that will impact your future fulfillment and security. The job? To successfully integrate your sexuality with the rest of your life. We want you to be the same person on Friday night that you are on Sunday when you are at church. We don't want you to live a Christian life in front of some people but then act differently around guys. A segmented life brings confusion, guilt, and often despair.

We don't want that for you. We want you to have a healthy view of sex. We want you to believe that sex as God intended it is so great that it's worth waiting until marriage to experience. We want you to be comfortable with yourself and with others, deeply connected, and free of guilt and shame. We want the best for you and hope this little book will be the beginning of your seeking, finding, and living the best life possible.

PART I

understanding
our battle

daring to be truthful

If you hold to my teaching, you are really my disciples. Then you will know the truth, and the truth will set you free.

JOHN 8:31-32

Truth or dare. You've probably played this game with girlfriends at a slumber party or perhaps been warned by your parents not to play it at all. It's a game where you agree to do anything another player dares you to do, regardless of how embarrassing or disgusting it may be, or else to tell the absolute truth in response to a particular question, regardless of how private or humiliating your answer may be.

As a young girl, I never opted out of playing such games. It never even occurred to me I had a choice. My friends dared me to do some ridiculous things—eat a ketchup, mustard, and mayonnaise sandwich; drink a Dr. Pepper as fast as possible and then burp as loudly as I could in front of my friend's older brother; and passionately kiss my stuffed monkey while my friend took a Polaroid picture. But I usually took the dare because I didn't want to answer questions such as these: Who do you think is the cutest boy in school? How many boys have you kissed? How far have you ever gone with a boy? Eating something gross or making an idiot out of myself was easy compared to telling the truth about certain things.

Sometimes the truth hurts, and it's much easier if we can keep it hidden. As a matter of fact, sometimes the secrets we harbor are so painful that we don't want to face them ourselves. We assume that these secrets will go away if we don't think or talk about them with anyone. But the opposite is true. Shameful secrets fester like a splinter in a finger, and it's much better to name the secret and to let someone help us remove it from our lives so the wound will heal.

You will read many stories in this book from young women (ages twelve to twenty) who have courageously done just that. They've dared to tell the truth about their battle to guard their minds, hearts, and bodies from sexual sin. We hope that you will learn some lessons the easy way and avoid making mistakes of your own, or that you will recognize the truth about any struggles you are currently facing in your battle for sexual purity and understand how you can overcome them.

IGNORANCE IS NOT A VIRTUE

You may find some of the stories in this book eyeopening or surprising. Please know that we are not trying to shock, disgust, or defile* you in any way. We want you to be wise to the ways of the world so you can guard yourself against them. Ignorance is not a spiritual gift, nor is it a virtue. You can be wise *and* innocent at the same time, and we intend to prepare you to make responsible decisions if and when temptations come across your path. Also, don't assume that the temptations we'll be discussing won't come to call in your life. The apostle Paul wrote:

> So, if you think you are standing firm, be careful that you don't fall!…
> Therefore, prepare your minds for action; be self-controlled.… Do not
> conform to the evil desires you had when you lived in ignorance. But
> just as he who called you is holy, so be holy in all you do; for it is written:
> "Be holy, because I am holy."… Among you there must not be even a
> hint of sexual immorality." (1 Corinthians 10:12; 1 Peter 1:13-16;
> Ephesians 5:3)

Let's peek into the private lives of some of your peers who were brave enough to tell the truth about their battles for sexual purity.

MOLLY'S PRIVATE WAR

Molly's struggle began when she stumbled upon a pornographic television show and later chose to stumble onto it again…and again…and again.

---

* *defile*—to corrupt one's purity

I know that it was wrong and that everyone messes up big time, but I still feel bad, mainly because I not only exposed myself to pornography,* but I also exposed two of my very best friends. One of them was a good enough friend to me to confess to her parents what we had done. My parents were extremely upset, and I don't blame them. They even helped me by having someone change the television settings so that nothing pornographic comes in now, and that channel is blank.

I was fine for a while and tried very hard to forget what I saw, which worked for the most part. But recently I have developed a habit of masturbating† to these images and cannot stop. I know this is wrong, and I feel dirty and guilty. I have confessed my sins to God, but that doesn't seem to be enough. I don't want anyone to find out, because I know that they would be disgusted and disappointed in me.

We're sure that if Molly had known how addicting pornography can be, she would have avoided it altogether. If either pornography or habitual masturbation have become problems in your life, this book will help you break free from these habits that hinder your sexual integrity and spiritual peace.

LAUREN'S PRIVATE WAR

Lauren attended a sexuality conference when she was in junior high and made a pledge to remain sexually abstinent until marriage. Now in high school, she is disheartened by the choices her friends are making and can't help but wonder if it's realistic for her to maintain her pledge.

I went to a dance at my school and most of my friends were freak dancing, moving around like they were having sex with their clothes on, and doing nasty stuff with each other—girls with guys, girls with girls, anything goes.

---

* *pornography*—material that graphically demonstrates sexually erotic behavior

† *masturbating*—touching one's own genitals in order to cause self-arousal

Everyone looked like they were having so much fun, and they kept telling me to lighten up and join the party. Also, a couple of my girlfriends accepted a dare to perform oral sex* on some guys in the back of the bus—and now those girls are *really* popular with the guys. I try to remind myself that they are popular for the wrong reasons, but sometimes I wonder if I'm being too prudish and am missing out on all the fun it seems that everyone else is having.

We know many of you reading this book want to maintain sexual purity, but like Lauren, you feel all alone in your desire and are wondering if it's even possible. Don't be discouraged. It's not only possible, but we believe you'll agree that it's much better to wait to enjoy sex according to God's perfect plan—in marriage someday—than to engage in sexual activities as if they're just another recreational hobby. Keep reading and we'll show you exactly how you can do just that.

EMMA'S PRIVATE WAR

Emma was daring enough to share the truth about her struggles in hopes of encouraging other young women to avoid the mistakes she made. She felt very insecure in her early teens and believed something was wrong with her because guys never seemed attracted to her. Even though she had good relationships with her parents, she wanted to be pursued by a young man. In order to make herself look more like the popular girls at school, she started dieting and exercising to lose weight.

It didn't take long for my weight loss obsession to turn into a serious eating disorder. I felt desperate for boys to notice my slender body, and I craved compliments like crazy. When a guy did compliment me, it puffed me up with pride and I felt like I was really something. I would hang around him more as some sort of "payment" for the attention he gave me as well as a "security deposit" so that he'd keep the compliments coming. I'd also flirt by linking arms with him buddy-style, bumping into him on purpose, or leaning up against him.

---

* *oral sex*—placing one's mouth on the partner's genital area for sexual stimulation

Over the next three years I got into a couple of relationships that I thought were serious, but the guys weren't so serious. I gave these guys all I had, including my body, but eventually I got dumped for the next girl. Every time I experienced another breakup, I wondered what was wrong with me. Why didn't he want me anymore? Was I not attractive enough? Was I still too fat? Abusing my body and giving it away was how I tried to get the attention and affirmation I wanted from a guy, but what I got was never enough.

The battle to be thin enough, as well as the battle to get your emotional needs met by any boyfriend, can seem like a never-ending one. If you've found yourself craving a relationship so much that you engage in behaviors you are not proud of, this book is for you. It will help you gain a healthy balance between your natural, God-given desire to be loved and your ability to avoid sexually tempting situations.

As a matter of fact, I wish I had known the information in this book when I was your age and fighting my own battles.

Shannon's Private War

If anyone had asked me when I was twelve if I wanted to remain a virgin until marriage, I would have said, "Of course I do!"

At thirteen, I would have said, "I think so."

By fourteen, I would have replied, "Maybe."

At age fifteen, my response would have been, "I don't see how that is possible." Unfortunately, my innocence became just a memory that year. I was date raped, which I never told anyone about for fear that I would be blamed. I had, after all, flirted with this eighteen-year-old boy to get his attention and had agreed to spend time alone with him behind my parents' back, so I mistakenly said nothing. Because I kept this secret, no one helped me heal from the abuse or told me I was still a virgin in God's eyes. (We'll talk more about the nature of virginity in the next chapter.)

A few months later, my parents allowed me to begin dating. Because I believed that my virginity had already been stolen from me, I didn't feel I had a reason to withhold my body from most of the young men I dated. Sex became a routine part of my romantic relationships—the price that I felt I must pay for the attention and affection that I craved. This is one of the reasons I want you to read this book. I want you to have information I did not have. I also want you to live without secrets and to be open about who you are and how you feel about boys and what they want to do with you.

NO EXEMPTIONS FROM SEXUAL TEMPTATION

As you read about the darker side of my younger days, you might think I was a messed-up girl from a dysfunctional home and a bad neighborhood, or that I wasn't a Christian, or that I wasn't too smart.

Wrong.

I grew up in rural Northeast Texas with educated, middle-class parents who were faithfully married to each other. My family lived in a modest home in the country where safety was never an issue. Mother took me to church regularly, and I confirmed my belief in Jesus Christ at the age of twelve. I even served as president of my youth group for several years. I got straight As in high school and went on to graduate from college.

As my life shows, you don't have to be messed up or even come from a messed-up family to make irresponsible decisions that will mess up your life. Not even "good Christian girls" are exempt from sexual temptations. Not even you.

What would cause someone like you or your friends to go from saving herself for her Prince Charming to kissing toads? Is it possible to climb out of the toad swamp once you are in it? Is this a war that can even be won? If so, how?

This book answers these questions. It will show you how you can maneuver through the minefield of youth without losing the battle for sexual and emotional integrity. If you can avoid the land mines and be victorious in the battle, you will be more likely to enter your adult years with confidence and purpose. Your life will be free of desperation, and you will make great choices for your future. The world can be yours, but first learn more about the intensity of your own private battle by answering yes or no to the following questions.

1. Do you watch television shows or movies with sexual jokes or graphic sex scenes?

2. Does the music you listen to talk blatantly of sexual desires outside of marriage?

3. Do you ever act overly friendly or seductively* to get a guy's attention?

4. Do thoughts of having or keeping a boyfriend consume your mind to the point that you find it difficult to concentrate on anything else for any length of time?

5. Are you looking for or entertaining the idea of a serious romantic relationship even though it will be several years before you are ready to get married?

6. Do you habitually masturbate to pleasure yourself sexually or as a means of resisting sexual involvement with others?

7. Do you consider oral sex or other sexual activities okay because they're not vaginal sex and you can't get pregnant from them?

8. Do you feel that your virginity has been stolen from you?

9. Do you feel as if you are "damaged goods" that a "respectable guy" wouldn't want?

10. Do you believe it is ever okay for a couple to live together even though they are not married?

11. Do you believe it is ever okay for a couple to have sex before marriage?

12. Have you ever lied to your parents about where you were going or whom you were with because you knew they wouldn't approve if you told the truth?

13. Would you lie to your parents in order to go out with a particular guy you liked a lot if you knew you could get away with it?

14. Have you ever made out with a guy just because it seemed like the thing to do?

15. Are you anxious to get out from under the control of your parents and gain your freedom to pursue any relationship you want?

16. Do you go into Web sites or chat rooms that you know your parents would not approve of?

---

* *seductively*—in an alluring or sexually tempting manner

17. Have you ever given your phone number or physical address to a stranger you were flirting with over the Internet without your parents' knowledge?

18. Have you set rules or guidelines for your behavior or your relationships that you've already broken?

19. Do you hide certain things, such as steamy love letters, magazines, or videos?

20. Do you envision that getting married someday will be the answer to all of your problems and relieve you of your sexual and emotional temptations?

Which questions did you mark yes? Each one reveals a potential pitfall that makes you more likely to give in to sexual temptation when it arises. Whether you are just entering puberty and new to this struggle or an experienced young adult, you can design a rock-solid defense to avoid becoming a casualty of this war. Whether you are sexually pure, hanging on to your virginity by a thread, or sleeping with a guy, you can maintain and/or reclaim your sexual integrity not just throughout your youth, but throughout your whole life. Recognizing and understanding what kind of things can cause every woman, regardless of her age or marital status, to stumble and fall into sexual temptation is the key. By learning to guard your mind, heart, and body against sexual compromise and understanding God's plan for your sexual and emotional fulfillment, you can maneuver your way through your teenage years with grace...and without regrets.

As you begin to understand this gift of sexuality more fully, you will be able to dispel some of the myths that can keep you entrenched in this battle. The coming chapters will help you

- understand the complexity of your sexuality and what part your emotions play in the battle;

- recognize the myths about sexuality that dominate our culture and how they can affect your sexual beliefs and choices;

- embrace sexual purity as a preferred lifestyle, not just physically, but mentally, emotionally, and spiritually as well;

- enjoy healthy, satisfying relationships with yourself, God, and others;

- find the love that you are looking for without looking in the wrong places or placing unrealistic expectations on your boyfriend or future husband; and

- feel good about yourself not just for a moment but for the rest of your life.

If you have been successful in overcoming temptations thus far, praise God for His protection, and prepare for further victory. If you have given in to any of these temptations, if you wonder why you feel so disconnected from God, or if you feel anxious about your present or future relationships, this book could be your pathway to peace.

Our prayer is that you will find wisdom, courage, hope, and strength to face *and win* the battle for sexual and emotional integrity.

 He holds victory in store for the upright, he is a shield to those whose walk is blameless, for he guards the course of the just and protects the way of his faithful ones. Then you will understand what is right and just and fair—every good path. For wisdom will enter your heart, and knowledge will be pleasant to your soul. Discretion will protect you, and understanding will guard you.

Proverbs 2:7-11

back to the blueprints for sexuality

So God created man in his own image...male and female he created
them.... God saw all that he had made, and it was very good.

GENESIS 1:27,31

If someone were to ask you, "What is sex?" how would you respond? If you are like
most people, you might blush and hem and haw until you manage to speak the
words "penis" and "vagina" and explain the mechanics of how babies are made. As
surprised as you may be to hear this, that answer is incorrect. You just defined *sexual intercourse.*

Think we're just being picky about the choice of words here? Well, the last time
you filled out a form at school and saw the word *sex* with a blank line next to it, did
you write "virgin" (or "nonvirgin")? Of course you didn't! You wrote "female." God
created us all to be sexual beings, either male or female. Our femininity or masculinity is an expression of who we are. We are sexual beings from the time we are
conceived until we die and leave our earthly bodies for our heavenly home. You
were sexual when you dressed your Barbie dolls, when you started shaving your
legs, and when you cried over your first broken heart. As a matter of fact, you are
being *sexual* right now as you read this book! Surprised? Believe us when we say
you don't have to be engaged in sexual activity to be sexual. You are a sexual human
being all the time, and that's something you cannot change.

However, your sexuality may not be fully integrated* into the rest of your per-

---

* *integrated*—formed or blended into a whole

sonality. You may have compartmentalized* your sexuality because you are ashamed of it or uncomfortable with it. If so, you might be very responsible at school and church, but when you are with a guy, you almost turn into another person. Your discomfort, insecurity, secrecy, or shame might lead you to impulsive† and irresponsible behavior. We want to help you integrate your sexuality so that you become a consistent, confident, whole, and healthy sexual person.

Upon hearing that you are a sexual person, you might think, *Well, if God made me to be a sexual being, He must intend for me to have sex!* But you are confusing being *sexual* with being *sexually active.* The two are *not* the same thing. By God's design we are sexual (male or female) all our lives, but His perfect plan only allows for sexual intercourse within the boundaries of a marriage relationship.

Or you might mistakenly believe, *Once I have sex, I'll be a woman. Until then, I'm still a girl.* Our society has almost made the act of sexual intercourse into a rite of passage into adulthood. It's not. In fact, that's complete nonsense.

Think about it. If a ten-year-old girl has sex, does that make her a woman? Statistically speaking, only 80 percent of women will ever marry, so does that mean the 20 percent who stay single remain girls rather than women? Does the fact that an adult has never had sex make that person any less of a man or a woman? Of course not. Having sex doesn't make you a man or a woman any more than standing in a garage holding a flower vase makes you a Volkswagen Beetle. In other words, your sexuality is defined not by *what you do,* but by *who you are.* By God's design, your female sexuality differs distinctly from a male's sexuality.

VIVE LA DIFFÉRENCE! (FRENCH FOR "CELEBRATE THE DIFFERENCE!")

When I brought my newborn son home from the hospital, it did not take long for my three-year-old daughter to declare, "Mommy! I don't have a penis!" The difference between our physical bodies is only the beginning of the differences

---

* *compartmentalized*—separated into different categories

† *impulsive*—acting momentarily without thought to consequences

between males and females. Understanding these differences is vital to guarding your sexual purity and helping others do the same.

Perhaps a trip back to the Garden of Eden will help.

Imagine Adam and Eve in the garden. God gives them the command, "Be fruitful and increase in number" (Genesis 1:28). This was a two-part command: have sex and make babies.

Now if Adam was so much like Eve that all he wanted to do was walk in the garden holding hands with his wife, pick flowers, and share his innermost thoughts and feelings, would they have ever gotten around to having sex? Probably not.

But God placed in Adam an ability to be turned on simply at the sight of Eve's extraordinary beauty so that he would want to obey God's command to "multiply and increase in number." One look at her feminine figure and he thought, *Whoa, Baby! Come to Papa!*[1]

God gave men the incredible responsibility of being the progenitors* of the human race (sounds like the title of an Arnold Schwarzenegger movie, doesn't it?). To equip man for such an enormous task, God placed in him exactly what he would need in order to fulfill his responsibility: the desire to be physically intimate and experience pleasure. A man longs to reach out and touch, fondle, embrace, and expel all his energies making love with the object of his affection.

Ever since Adam first laid eyes on Eve, males have been very stimulated by what they take in through their eyes. When visually stimulated, a guy's sperm† production kicks into high gear, boosting his craving for physical touch to levels which can make him feel very out of control. However, with God's help every male can learn to control these sexual desires and prove that he is a man, not just a male animal.

Now if all Eve wanted to do was chase Adam and have sex, work in the fields, arm wrestle, and play football, would she have raised healthy, well-balanced, sensitive children? Probably not. (Never mind what her son Cain turned out like, just go along with me!)

But God placed in Eve the desire to be emotionally connected and involved in

---

* *progenitor*—forefather or originator

† *sperm*—reproductive cells produced in a male's testicles that can fertilize the female egg and result in pregnancy.

caring for and nurturing others. God wanted her to obey His command to "be fruitful" or to "make grow." He gave her, and all females, the responsibility of being the nurturers of the human race, and He placed in her exactly what she would need to fulfill that responsibility: the desire to be emotionally intimate. A woman is made to cradle, caress, converse with, and care for the object of her affection.

So while young men are primarily aroused by what they see with their eyes, as a young woman you are more aroused by what you hear and feel. The temptation to look at pornography can be overwhelming to a guy, but you may be more likely to read a romance novel or go gaga over a rock star. A male may fantasize about watching a woman undress, but you would be more likely to fantasize about a guy whispering sweet nothings in your ear while touching you gently. A male wants to look and touch, while you would prefer to relate and connect emotionally.

While a guy gets tempted sexually because of what he sees, you are more likely to be tempted sexually because your heart is crying out for someone to satisfy your innermost desires to be loved, needed, valued, and cherished. While a guy also needs mental, emotional, and spiritual connection, his physical needs tend to be in the driver's seat and his other needs ride along in the back. The reverse is true for you. A young woman's emotions are usually in the driver's seat. That's why it's said that guys *give love to get sex* and girls *give sex to get love.* Sadly, we know of many girls who had sex when all they really wanted was someone to hold them. We want you to know that sex outside of marriage will never bring you the love and acceptance you want, but with God's help you can find fulfillment and satisfaction in healthy ways.

In addition, a male can enjoy the act of sex without committing his heart or bonding spiritually with the object of his physical desire. This is the ultimate act of compartmentalization, and guys are masters at it. Never assume a guy feels what you feel.

A healthy young female, on the other hand, usually gives her body only to someone she thinks of night and day and with whom her heart and spirit have already connected (unless there is dysfunctional or addictive behavior involved). And when she gives her mind, heart, and soul, her body usually follows right behind them. The four are intricately connected.

Every Young Man's Battle, which Steve coauthored with Fred Stoeker, discusses how important it is for guys to "bounce" their eyes (immediately look away at something else) to avoid looking at a woman lustfully. While you also need to guard your eyes (women can be visually stimulated as well), your primary concern needs to be guarding your heart and "bouncing" your thoughts (immediately turning your thoughts away from the temptation to focus on something else).

Figure 2.1 shows a quick recap of the differences we've just discussed.

Later on we'll talk about some other differences between guys and girls, but for now the most important thing for you to understand is that God created males and females to be very different. Yet as different as we are, we fit together perfectly.

CREATED FOR CONNECTION

Part of God's perfect plan is that we are so physically, mentally, emotionally, and spiritually drawn to the opposite sex that we long for closeness with each other—not just an "I want to sit beside you" closeness, but a deep desire to be intimately connected.

Intimacy can best be defined by breaking the word into its syllables: "in-to-me-see." The longing for connection with the opposite sex is a longing to be seen and accepted for who we really are deep down inside, as well as to see the other person deep inside so that we truly know each other. As a matter of fact, according to Webster's dictionary, one of the definitions of the word *know* is "to have sexual intercourse with."

God designed the male and female bodies so that the penis fits perfectly inside the vagina during the act of sexual intercourse. But sexual intercourse was not intended to be just a *physical* connection. God designed sexual intercourse to be shared between two bodies, two minds, two hearts, and two spirits that unite to become a one-flesh union. When this level of intimacy is experienced within the commitment and safety of a loving marriage, it can be one of the most earthshaking and fulfilling experiences you'll ever know this side of heaven. God wants you to enjoy sex, and that is why He gave you a body part, the clitoris,* that has no other purpose but to give you sexual pleasure. Yay, God!

---

* *clitoris*—a small organ located toward the front of the vaginal area which provides pleasure when aroused or stimulated

PERFECTLY DESIGNED TO BE WORTH THE WAIT

Amazing, isn't it? Our God designed males and females to fit together perfectly, to long for emotional connection with one another, and to be stimulated and aroused by the sights, sounds, and even smells of one another. He loves us so much that He designed every fiber of our being to want to fulfill His commandment to be fruitful and multiply. He created the act of sexual intimacy as a means to provide men and women with physical, mental, emotional, and spiritual pleasure beyond description.

So if sex is so wonderful, why shouldn't you be allowed to engage in sexual activity as soon as you feel ready? as soon as you experience the longing for intimacy and closeness? as soon as your hottie radar goes off?

Because God's perfect plan is that you enjoy sexual intercourse exclusively within marriage. As much as God knows the pleasures of sex and the bonding that can take place when a couple engages in it, He also knows the painful consequences of sex outside of marriage—physical, mental, emotional, and spiritual consequences that you'll read about throughout this book—and He wants to protect you from those. The great sex you and your husband will enjoy someday will be free from painful consequences or guilt—and well worth the wait!

Imagine what it is like when two sexually pure people get married. He has guarded his heart and bounced his eyes, and she is the only naked woman he has ever seen. Can you imagine how hot she would be to him? And she has never been held so intimately that she knows the smell of any man's skin but his. She has no

GUYS	GIRLS
• driven by their physical desires	• driven by their emotional desires
• crave physical intimacy	• crave emotional intimacy
• stimulated by what they see	• stimulated by what they hear and feel
• give love to get sex	• give sex to get love
• body can disconnect from mind, heart, and spirit	• body, mind, heart and spirit intricately connected

Figure 2.1

one to compare his gentle touch and caress to. Can you imagine how hot he would be to her? They can have guilt-free sex however many times in whatever way they want until they die. Now that is what God wants sex to be. No comparison. No disappointment. No guilt or shame. Only good, clean fun between husband and wife.

 For this reason a man will leave his father and mother and be united to his wife, and they will become one flesh. The man and his wife were both naked, and they felt no shame.

Genesis 2:24-25

building lives
of sexual integrity

> Dear friends, build yourselves up in your most holy faith and pray in
> the Holy Spirit. Keep yourselves in God's love.
>
> JUDE 20-21

On an episode of the sitcom *My Wife and Kids,* Michael (Damon Wayans) and
Janet (Tisha Campbell-Martin) argue about whether to allow their teenage daughter to go out on her first date with a particular young man. Michael says to his
wife, "I just don't want this boy to cross the line with my daughter."

His wife asks, "What line?" to which he responds, "The panty line!"

Unfortunately, the panty line is exactly where too many young women envision
sexual integrity to stop and compromise to start. But is the panty line really where
compromise begins? Obviously, we don't think so.

INTEGRITY VS. COMPROMISE

In the previous chapter we discussed how God created us to be sexual beings and
that He intends for sex to be shared and enjoyed only within the marriage relationship. With that in mind, we're ready to talk about sexual integrity. To be a person
of integrity means that you are undivided—that all parts of your life line up with
the other parts. People who believe in Jesus Christ and claim to be Christians will
strive to live a life that lines up with all of Jesus' teachings. When successful in living such a life, they display integrity.

If you think being a person of sexual integrity means that you are a boring,
frigid young woman who never has any fun with a guy, nothing can be further
from the truth. A young woman of sexual integrity is free to enjoy the excitement

and fun of a romantic relationship without all the worry that compromise brings into our lives.

Compromise is the opposite of integrity. It leads you to do things that take your mind and heart away from Christ. It usually begins in small ways but eventually blossoms into big-time sin that controls you.

So if you want to live a life of sexual integrity, you will be undivided in your devotion to sexual purity, refusing to be controlled by your sexual passions. When you exercise self-control, you will be free to share yourself completely with your husband in a passionate sexual relationship without the scars and emotional baggage that can come with compromise. Just think how much your husband will love that you saved your sexual pleasures especially for him and that you can love him with reckless abandon, not just with your body, but also your mind, heart, and soul.

TABLETOP SEXUALITY

To better understand the meaning of sexual integrity, think of your sexuality as a table. Just as a table is comprised of four legs that give it balance, our sexuality is also comprised of four distinct components that bring balance to our lives. If one of the legs of a table is missing or broken, the table easily loses its balance and becomes a slide instead.

> "By reading this book I've had my eyes opened to the fact that girls have their own sexual struggles just like guys do. I've never realized the difficulties girls have in guarding their hearts, so hopefully I'll stop and think about that when I'm tempted to flirt with them in the future."
>
> —JOHN

My friends Kevin and Ruth discovered this concept at their wedding reception. A long lace-covered banquet table displayed the beautiful multitiered wedding cake, the crystal punch bowl and cups, sterling silverware, and froufrou monogrammed napkins. The only problem was that whoever set up the table had forgotten to fasten the latch on one of the folding legs. As soon as the red punch was poured into the crystal punch bowl, the leg buckled and everything slid down to the end of the table and onto the floor with a clatter! The cake toppled into the pool of red punch and the napkins were soaked. Everyone looked to the bride and groom, expecting shock and horror. To everyone's delight, however, Kevin and Ruth broke out into hysterical laughter!

But it's no laughing matter when one of the legs of your sexuality buckles, because then your life can become a slippery slope leading to discontentment, sexual compromise, self-loathing, and emotional brokenness. When this happens, God's blessing, intended to bring richness and pleasure to your life, feels more like a curse that brings great pain and despair.

As we mentioned, your sexuality is comprised of four distinct aspects: the physical, mental, emotional, and spiritual dimensions of your being. These four parts combine to form the unique individual God designed you to be. Again, your sexuality isn't *what you do.* Your sexuality is *who you are,* and you are made with a body, mind, heart, and spirit, not just a body. So, sexual integrity is not just about remaining physically abstinent. It is about purity in all four aspects of your being—body, mind, heart, and spirit. When all four aspects line up perfectly, your "tabletop" (your sexuality) reflects balance and integrity.

UNIDENTIFIED SLIPPERY SLOPES

Many young women would call themselves sexually pure simply because they've never had sexual intercourse or because they've never let a guy go beyond their panty line. Are they correct? Consider these questions:

- Perhaps you have never kissed a boy, but you look at pornography, read steamy romance novels, or listen to sexually suggestive music and mentally fantasize about fooling around or going all the way with someone you are not married to. Can you honestly say that you are living a life of sexual integrity? (This is an example of mental compromise.)
- Perhaps you are a "physical virgin," but have repeatedly used guys to try to get the affirmation you crave. Can it be said that you are living a life of sexual integrity? (This is an example of emotional compromise.)
- Perhaps you wear a True Love Waits ring or necklace, but the only reason you go to youth group is to scope out the cute guys, not to know God

better. Can you sincerely say you have your priorities straight? (This is an example of spiritual compromise.)

• Maybe you've never had intercourse, but you've allowed a guy to put his hand up your shirt or you've given a guy a hand job* or a blow job.† Can you honestly say that you are still sexually pure? (This is an example of physical compromise.)

In order to experience the physical, mental, emotional, and spiritual stability that God intends for you to have, you must avoid turning your tabletop into a slippery slope through some sort of compromise. If you are wondering how to accomplish this, rest assured that by the time you get to the end of this book, you will have the answers.

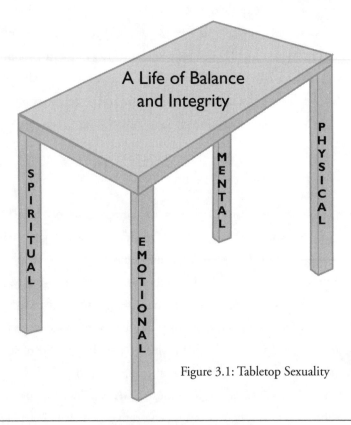

Figure 3.1: Tabletop Sexuality

---

* *hand job*—slang term for massaging a male's penis with your hand

† *blow job*—slang term for a female performing oral sex on a male

Until you are married, sexual integrity means protecting yourself from any physical, mental, emotional, or spiritual longings for the opposite sex that cannot be fulfilled according to God's plan. It means looking to God to satisfy these needs until they can be fulfilled in a marriage relationship. It doesn't mean you can't be interested in or hopeful of having a husband someday or that you can't date or have a boyfriend. It simply means that you try your best to guard your heart, mind, and body against any compromise that threatens your sexual integrity.

When you marry, sexual integrity will equate to intimately connecting physically, mentally, emotionally, and spiritually with your husband and no other man outside your marriage. Any compromise whatsoever—physical, mental, emotional, or spiritual—will affect your sexual integrity as a whole. One infected part will eventually infect all of its corresponding parts or, at the very least, rob you of the sexual wholeness and fulfillment that God longs for you to have.

LEGALISM VS. LOVE

When it comes to sexual integrity, most people want a list of dos and don'ts, cans and can'ts, shoulds and shouldn'ts. They want to know: *What can I get away with? How far can I go? What's too far?* However, a list of laws about what we can and can't wear, should and should not do and say, and so on, isn't the best answer, because these guidelines only address our physical actions. But what about our motivations and thoughts when we select our clothes or choose what behaviors are appropriate or inappropriate in a relationship? You need a standard of sexual integrity that will address not just physical behaviors, but emotional and mental behaviors as well. How can we develop a set of rules that will cover our minds, hearts, *and* bodies?

The answer lies not in legalism, which is defined as "abiding by a set of strict laws," but in Christian love. God boiled the many rules and regulations set out in the Old Testament down to just ten commandments. Then in the New Testament, Jesus reduced all those laws down to only two. If you live by these two commandments, you will live a life of sexual integrity.

These two laws are explained when Jesus responded to the question, Which is the greatest commandment?

"Love the Lord your God with all your heart and with all your soul and with
all your mind." This is the first and greatest commandment. And the second
is like it: "Love your neighbor as yourself." All the Law and the Prophets
hang on these two commandments. (Matthew 22:37-40)

Jesus was saying that the law isn't what is important—love is. If you love God,
love your neighbor, and love yourself (in that order), then you can live far above
any set of rules or regulations. When you live by the spirit of love, you are free from
any legalistic standards.

Paul echoed this form of "freedom with responsibility" when he wrote:

"Everything is permissible"—but not everything is beneficial. "Everything
is permissible"—but not everything is constructive. Nobody should seek his
own good, but the good of others. (1 Corinthians 10:23-24)

Paul was saying, "You can do most anything, but it isn't always in your best
interest or in the interest of others. Focus not on what is 'allowed,' but on what is
best for all involved." How does this apply to sexual integrity?

Pick any issue and sift it through this law vs. love filter:

- There is no law against flattering clothes, but is your motive in wearing
  them to build others up or to build up your own ego by turning a guy's
  head?
- We have freedom of speech in this country, but are the things you say to
  guys in their best interest or are your words merely a tool to manipulate
  them into giving you the attention you crave?
- The Bible doesn't prohibit French kissing, but is it a loving thing to do to
  get a guy's juices flowing (not to mention your own), awakening sexual
  desires that shouldn't be satisfied outside of marriage?

Look beyond the movements to the motivations behind your actions. By doing
this, you no longer have to concern yourself with the law because you are acting by
a higher standard, a standard of love. The columns of Figure 3.2, comparing questions of compromise to questions of integrity, show the difference between evaluat-

ing your motives and behaviors through the lens of legalism vs. evaluating them through the lens of love.

God holds each of us accountable to do what we know to do. If you want to be a young woman of sexual integrity, you may need to let go of some of your freedoms (in dress, thoughts, speech, and behavior) in order to serve the best interest of others out of love. Not only will God provide this knowledge of how to act with integrity, He will also honor you if you apply this knowledge and act with responsibility.

A Young Woman of Sexual and Emotional Integrity

Let's put this all together. If you want to be a young woman of sexual and emotional integrity, make sure that your thoughts, words, emotions, and actions reflect an inner beauty and a sincere love for God, others, and yourself. Not that you will never be tempted to think, say, feel, or do something inappropriate, but you will try diligently to resist these temptations and stand firm in your convictions. You won't use the opposite sex in an attempt to get your emotional cravings met, nor will you entertain sexual fantasies. You won't dress to seek male attention, but you won't limit your wardrobe to ankle-length skirts and turtleneck sweaters, either. You'll dress

Questions of Compromise *Don't Ask*	Questions of Integrity *Do Ask*
• Are my actions lawful?	• Are my actions loving to others?
• Will anyone find out?	• Is this something I'd be proud of?
• Would anyone condemn me?	• Is this my highest standard?
• Is this socially acceptable?	• Is this in line with my convictions?
• Are my clothes too revealing?	• Am I dressing for attention?
• How can I get what I want?	• What is my motive for wanting this?
• Can I get away with saying this?	• Would this be better left unsaid?
• Will this hurt anyone?	• Will this benefit others?

Figure 3.2

fashionably and look sharp and maybe even appear sexy to a guy (like beauty, "sexy" is in the eye of the beholder, and some guys will think you look sexy even when you dress modestly), but your motivation won't be self-seeking or seductive. You will present yourself as an attractive young woman because you know you represent God to others.

Your life will line up with your lip. If you claim to be a follower of Christ, you won't disregard His many teachings on sexual immorality, lustful thoughts, immodest dress, and inappropriate talk. You will live what you believe about God, and your beauty will shine from the inside out. Finally, you will have an incredible hope for your future marriage—that it will be everything God intended for it to be, especially the passionate sexual relationship you and your husband will be able to enjoy.

If you are ready to discover more about how you can live a life of sexual integrity, guarding not just your body but your mind and heart as well, keep reading as we dispel some of the myths that can keep you entrenched in this battle.

 Therefore everyone who hears these words of mine and puts them into practice is like a wise man who built his house on the rock. The rain came down, the streams rose, and the winds blew and beat against that house; yet it did not fall, because it had its foundation on the rock. But everyone who hears these words of mine and does not put them into practice is like a foolish man who built his house on sand. The rain came down, the streams rose, and the winds blew and beat against that house, and it fell with a great crash.

Matthew 7:24-27

myths that intensify our struggle

My people are destroyed from lack of knowledge.

HOSEA 4:6

Each year I teach hundreds of teens and college-age women about how to over-come their tendencies to "look for love in all the wrong places." Some of these young women have experimented with sexual relationships in the past. At the end of each class, I ask participants to answer this question: What were the myths that you previously believed about sex, relationships, or dating that placed you in com-promising sexual situations or unhealthy relationships? The seven myths described in this chapter reflect the most common answers I receive.

Although at first glance you may think that a particular misconception doesn't apply to you, we encourage you to read about it anyway. We are often unaware of our personal beliefs about things we've not yet experienced. If you understand these myths and the lies they are based on, you'll have a stronger defense if and when you're tempted in one of these areas.

MYTH 1

How I dress is my business. It shouldn't be a concern for God or guys.

Before you believe that your wardrobe isn't an issue with God, try this scripture on for size:

> Jesus said to his disciples: "Things that cause people to sin are bound to
> come, but woe to that person through whom they come. It would be better

for [her] to be thrown into the sea with a millstone tied around [her] neck than for [her] to cause [another] to sin." (Luke 17:1-2)

Remember what was said earlier about what stimulates guys sexually? It's what they take in through their eyes! When guys see something sexually stimulating, such as a young woman dressed immodestly, their natural tendency is to lust after her and entertain thoughts of becoming sexual with her. It doesn't matter whether the guy is a Christian or not. Even godly guys can be visually tempted to lust. If you want to avoid causing your brothers to stumble and fall, you'll dress modestly.

Many young women, including Christians, wear skimpy spaghetti-strap tanks that showcase their breasts, sport miniskirts or short shorts that don't leave much to the imagination, or appear in cropped tops with low-rise jeans and bare midriffs, perhaps with thong underwear peeking out of the back. These same young women then complain, "Girls wouldn't have to fight so hard to say no if guys weren't trying so hard to make out with them!"

We asked Nate, a college student, to comment on this, and he said, "Guys wouldn't try so hard [to pursue girls sexually] if girls didn't dress like that's what they want! When guys see a girl wearing tight-fitting or revealing clothing, sure it makes our babe radar go off, and we take notice. But we're not thinking that she's marriage material or anything. If a guy has integrity, he'll look away and ignore her. If he doesn't, he's going to pursue her, but for all the wrong reasons." Well said, Nate. Thanks for dispelling this myth!

MYTH 2

All flirting is okay.

You may think it's always okay to flirt, but that may be because you don't understand what inappropriate flirting feels like to a guy. Letting a boy know that you are interested in a more meaningful relationship with him is one thing, but inappropriate flirting, which can also be called "teasing" or "seduction," is another. Should you emotionally or physically stir up a guy if you have no intention of pursuing a relationship with him? Is it loving to tease someone with your attentions and affections if you have no desire to fulfill any hopes you may arouse in him? In our opinion, showing a sincere love and respect for others allows no room for acting as if you are interested in being sexual with a guy when, in fact, you are not.

It is said that "actions speak louder than words," but we can never discount the effect that words alone can have on other people and on our own integrity. James 3:5-6 says, "Likewise the tongue is a small part of the body, but it makes great boasts. Consider what a great forest is set on fire by a small spark. The tongue also is a fire, a world of evil among the parts of the body. It corrupts the whole person, sets the whole course of his life on fire." If you want to avoid setting a guy's lust aflame and to keep your own passions in check, do yourself a favor and choose your words and actions wisely. Show your interest in a particular guy with an appropriate glance, smile, or friendly comment, but be sure you are not stirring up desires within him that should not be fulfilled until marriage.

MYTH 3

I need to have a boyfriend to feel as if I am "somebody." Having a boyfriend will solve all my problems.

Newsflash. If you think you *need* a boyfriend, you are *not ready* for a boyfriend. Contrary to the movie scenes you may have witnessed where one character declares to the other, "You complete me!" no human being can ever complete another. Only God can "complete" you. Yet many young women try with all their power to find that special someone who will make them feel as if life is really worth living (as if living as a satisfied single person isn't possible).

If either of the above statements describes you, we have some advice for you. Do yourself a favor and get a life! Not the fairy-tale life you are dreaming of where you meet a wonderful guy, fall in love, and live happily ever after in la-la land. You need to live in reality and recognize who God made you to be, and then do your best at being that person.

"But what if I don't like who I am?" you may ask. Perhaps you feel awkward, shy, or even ugly. Perhaps you desperately wish you could be someone else. With God's help, you can learn to accept the things you cannot change about yourself but change the things that you can. Don't focus so much on the little, temporary things, such as the guy who doesn't know you exist or the recurring zits on your nose. Take a step back and look at the bigger picture. What do you dream about doing with your life? What are your educational, career, social service, or ministry goals? Pursue those dreams and goals with passion. You'll develop a sense of who God made you to be, and you'll even grow to like that person, regardless of whether a guy notices you or how badly your face breaks out.

Why is getting a real life and pursuing personal goals so important? Because a boyfriend or husband will never make you completely happy. Period. It doesn't matter how good-looking, rich, athletic, smart, godly, or charming he may be. No man can ever make you feel like you are somebody. That comes from knowing how special you are to God and from becoming the person God created you to be. Become that person, and you will never have to look to a guy to make you happy. You won't need to, because you'll be delighted with yourself and with your life.

It's also true that the better person you become, the better person you'll attract. If you are a godly, goal-oriented individual, you are going to attract the same. But if your life amounts to nothing but finding someone to fill that vacuum in your soul, you are going to attract another desperate person. The two of you will be like two ticks without a dog, just sucking the lifeblood out of each other. And if you think you had problems before, just wait until you try to navigate through the muddy waters of a dysfunctional relationship!

Look, we know that being unattached has its own set of problems. Sometimes you feel lonely. You worry about what other people think of you. You contemplate your future and you fear that you'll be alone forever. But guess what? Having a relationship doesn't rid you of all your problems, either. You are only exchanging one set of problems for a different set of problems. When you are attached, you lose the freedom of doing your own thing. You can't plan your own future because you have this other person to consider, and you still worry about what other people think of you.

You might think that one-half of a person added to one-half of another person equals one whole relationship, but this isn't true. Two people in a relationship multiply the positive and negative factors of each other. If you are wounded and incomplete, you will attract the same, and the two of you will experience a mere fraction of what God intended—and a whole lot of what was not.

We hope you don't think we're down on dating or relationships. We're definitely not. Healthy dating relationships can be great, and marriage is truly wonderful. But a good relationship is more about *becoming* the right person than *finding* the right person. A healthy marriage is the union of two *already complete* people who choose to invest in each other. Two people who drain each other because they have nothing to invest—only withdrawals to take from each other—make for a very unhealthy, unfulfilling relationship.

MYTH 4

Guys want basically the same thing from dating relationships that girls want.

Just in case you didn't catch it before, let us say this loud and clear: Guys are motivated by an entirely different set of factors than girls are. Most of the time guys give *love* to get *sex,* but girls give *sex* to get *love.* Do you see what a dangerous combination this can be? If not, maybe the following example can help you understand more clearly. Seventeen-year-old Kristie explains:

> I thought Daniel and I were on the same page. I wanted a close, intimate relationship, but I also wanted to save sex until marriage. He said he wanted the same thing, but when we got alone behind closed doors, Daniel didn't want to talk long before making his move on me. For a while I was happy with just talking and kissing. I had no intention of going any further, but eventually his hands began to roam, and he got my motor running to the point that I allowed him to do things that I'm not proud of. I didn't have sex with him, but I came dangerously close, because I felt as if I needed to give him the physical closeness he wanted in order to get him to stay interested in me.

Kristie should have known better than to be alone with Daniel behind closed doors once he began pressuring her to do things physically that she didn't want to do. If you are naive enough to remain in this position (and we hope you aren't), you'll soon discover that talking and bonding emotionally isn't on the top of most young men's list of priorities. We're not saying that guys are pigs who only want sex. Many know their own vulnerabilities well enough to know better than to take a young woman behind closed doors if they aren't able to control their sexual desires. But we are saying that God wired guys differently. They are built for visual stimulation. Their ultimate goal is physical intimacy. It's just how they are made. It's not that they don't value or want emotional bonding; many do. But it isn't their ultimate goal.

On the other hand, you, as a female, are built for relational stimulation. Your ultimate goal is emotional bonding. It's just how you're made. When it becomes obvious that a guy wants more physically than you can give with a clear conscience, it's time to recognize that this relationship is not one that is honoring to you or to God.

MYTH 5

My love will save him. I can change him.

Don't make the mistake of dating a guy who needs some major repair work before you could consider him marriage material. Many young women are drawn to a guy's wild, rebellious side and then set out on a mission to mold him into the kind of man they really want him to be. We hate to break it to you, but you can't change or save anyone. Only God is in the business of doing that successfully. The research has already been done. A woman's love does not change a broken man's behavior. It only validates it. Her love says to him, "You are okay the way you are!"

When a young woman attempts to be her boyfriend's savior, she often gets hurt big time. In his book *The Biblical Basis of Christian Counseling for People Helpers,* Gary Collins gives us insight into this reality as he explains the "messiah complex":

> The *messiah complex* refers to the tendency for caring people…to become res-
> cuers who try to deliver others from their problems and difficult life circum-
> stances. At times, almost all of us want to be like messiahs, saving people

from their dysfunctional families, enslaving addictions, or self-destructive lifestyles.…

[But when people] try to be rescuers, the rescuers almost always end up being hurt. Even so, [we are] still tempted at times to be like a messiah. [A friend states,] "It would be nice if I could rescue people from their pain and release them from their problems…but whenever I am tempted to try taking on that role, I remember how powerless I am and I think about what happened to the real Messiah. He was crucified."[1]

If you don't care to be crucified emotionally in a dating relationship, leave the saving and changing of others to the Lord. Instead, simply pray for guys who have a lot of growing up and changing to do before they can be considered good marriage material.

Remember, what you date is what you are going to marry. Be sure that the young men you date do not need a character overhaul, by you or anyone else.

MYTH 6

I feel so sexually tempted, I must already be guilty, so why bother resisting?

Satan loves to use false guilt, convincing us to cross the line between temptation and sin with thoughts like these:

- You can't deny that you want him! You may as well go after him!
- You've already gone this far, what's one step further?
- He already knows how you really are, so there's no use pretending to be a goody two-shoes!

Satan uses thoughts like these to cause you to feel guilty, but your guilt is *false* guilt because you have not yet acted on your thoughts. You have been tempted to sin, but you have not yet sinned.

When Jesus taught that thinking upon sexual things is just as sinful as doing them (see Matthew 5:27-28), He was referring to entertaining sexual thoughts over and over or intentionally fantasizing about someone in sexual ways. There are thoughts that pop into our minds simply because we are human, but we don't have to entertain them or focus on them. We can distract ourselves and resist these thoughts, just as we can resist any temptation. Just as guys can learn to bounce their eyes away from things they should not see, you can learn to bounce your thoughts away from things you should not dwell on. Remember that temptation, in and of itself, is *not* sin. There's nothing to feel guilty about when you are tempted. If you don't believe us, maybe you will believe the writer of Hebrews when he says:

> For we do not have a high priest who is unable to sympathize with our weaknesses, but we have one who has been tempted in every way, just as we are—yet was without sin. Let us then approach the throne of grace with confidence, so that we may receive mercy and find grace to help us in our time of need. (Hebrews 4:15-16)

Did you get that? Jesus Himself was tempted in every way! *Even sexually?* you're thinking. Why not sexually? He was a man in every sense of the word. He had beautiful women following Him around. He was reaching out to minister to women who would have loved to have Him hold them in His arms. The writer didn't say, "He was tempted in every way except sexually." Jesus was human, and He experienced every human temptation. He set the example for us that just because we are sexually tempted, it does not mean that we must give in to our passions.

MYTH 7

There's no one who would really understand my struggle.

We believe this myth exists because, fearing judgment, girls usually don't openly discuss their sex lives with other females. Unfortunately, these fears are often confirmed very early in childhood. For instance, one girl tells a friend about her secret crush on a boy in their class. The friend inevitably whispers the secret to two other friends, or worse, tells the boy all about the girl's confession. If you went through experiences like these, you may have learned to guard your deepest, darkest secrets from other females.

Some girls grow up with guys as their best friends because they feel so strongly that other girls simply cannot be trusted. Many also find out the hard way that confiding in guys can be *more* dangerous than confiding in a girlfriend. All a girl can do is betray your confidence. A guy can take advantage of your vulnerability and make you his next sexual target if you aren't standing firm in your convictions.

Young women also tend not to be open about their sexual struggles because of the humiliation that comes with giving sex in order to get love. While some may brag about the fact that they're having sex with a particular guy, most don't brag about the total number of sexual partners they've had. That's because for a woman, the relationship is the prize; the sex was simply the price she had to pay to get the prize. If she paid the price but still didn't get the prize, she feels an incredible amount of humiliation in the realization that her body wasn't enough to keep him interested. Who wants to announce to the world that kind of shame?

It's our hope that if you know how common these issues are to young women, you won't hesitate to discuss your own sexual struggles with a trusted adult or a mature Christian girlfriend. We believe that 99.9 percent of all women face sexual temptations in varying degrees.

Paul tells us in 1 Corinthians 10:13: "No temptation has seized you except what is common to [woman]. And God is faithful; he will not let you be tempted beyond what you can bear. But when you are tempted, he will also provide a way out so that you can stand up under it." Paul didn't say, "If you experience sexual temptation, there must be something wrong with you because no one else struggles with it that much." He said that all temptations are "common." And because God creates all human beings (regardless of gender, nationality, or economic background) as sexual human beings, you can bet that sexual and relational temptations are by far the most common temptations on the planet.

What is the "way out" that God usually provides so that you can stand up under the temptation? Does He turn off your emotions altogether? No. An effective "way out" can come through the wise counsel of a trusted Christian mentor, such as a youth pastor or Sunday school teacher, or an accountability* friendship

---

* *accountability*—being answerable to another person who challenges you to make sure you stay on the right track

with a like-minded girlfriend who can encourage you to stand firm in the face of battle. Give this trusted confidant permission to ask you hard, personal questions, such as: Have you done things with your boyfriend that arouse sexual desires in either of you? Have you spoken flirtatious words that would turn a guy on? Have you entertained sexual fantasies or looked at pornography?

If you invite someone to hold you accountable like this, you will likely be more faithful about examining the condition of your heart and mind than if you harbor these things within yourself. When you fail to live up to God's standards, a wise mentor or an accountability friend can sharpen you, not with harsh judgment but with a reminder to use good judgment.

PREPARING FOR VICTORY

If you have believed any of these myths, we hope this chapter helped you recognize that you are standing in the line of fire in this struggle for sexual integrity. Please keep reading, as we will be discussing more truths that can help you dispel these myths and prepare you to guard your mind, heart, and body in our sex-saturated world.

If you love me, you will obey what I command. And I will ask the Father, and he will give you another Counselor to be with you forever—the Spirit of truth. The world cannot accept him, because it neither sees him nor knows him. But you know him, for he lives with you and will be in you.

John 14:15-17

PART II

avoiding self-destruction

fueling your own sexual fire

> Dear friends, I urge you, as aliens and strangers in the world, to abstain
> from sinful desires, which war against your soul.
>
> 1 PETER 2:11

God gave us many awesome gifts. Fire is one of them. Fire allows us to heat our homes, cook our food, and sterilize instruments. It also provides us with a great amount of enjoyment as we snuggle around a warm fireplace on a cold winter evening.

But despite fire's many benefits, it can also be very dangerous—just ask the hundreds of people who lost their homes to the fires that raged out of control for weeks in Southern California. Or ask a woman we know who was burning some leaves and threw some gasoline on the fire to speed up the process, setting off an explosion significant enough to cause third-degree burns over most of her legs. Failing to understand or respect the destructive potential of fire can cause great pain rather than pleasure.

Why all this talk about fire? Because it can help you understand another of God's awesome gifts: sexual desire. The hunger for sexual connection can be both pleasurable and functional, but it can also be dangerous if you don't respect it and fuel it unnecessarily. When used properly within the boundaries God established for sex—only within marriage—a woman's sexual desires draw her toward her husband for a deeper level of emotional connection and physical pleasure than she can find in any other earthly relationship.

However, many people give in to the temptation of fueling those sexual desires long before they are married or even in any type of romantic relationship. How?

Through masturbation or self-gratification. As you listen to what several of your peers have to say on this topic, we believe you'll come to see that masturbation doesn't quench any sexual fires, but actually fuels them.

TRUE CONFESSIONS

A friend who was spending the night with Heather introduced her to masturbation when she was in the sixth grade. Little did she know that this act would lead to a twelve-year addiction that eroded her self-esteem.

> I feel like I cannot control myself, and it brings so much guilt. I struggle with sexual thoughts and get turned on just by thinking about masturbat ing. I have taken this before the Lord so many times. What can I do? This has been something that makes me feel so dirty and inferior, but even know- ing this doesn't seem to be enough to make me stop.

Sometimes masturbation blossoms into a greater temptation to become sexu- ally active. Denise confesses that she used to masturbate as a practical way to avoid acting out sexually with others. But that plan eventually backfired on her.

> Whenever I masturbated before a date, I'd often think throughout the evening about how unsatisfied I still felt. I often gave in and had sex out of disappointment with the masturbation experience. Then I felt guilty about both.

This information may be surprising to you if you never knew that touching yourself in sexual ways could be wrong. Such was the case for Emily, who explains in an e-mail:

> I have been struggling with masturbation since I was very young. I didn't even know it was wrong or anything. As I have grown older (I'm seventeen), it has become the thing I most despise about myself.

I have never told anyone about my struggle. If I ever did, they would probably think I was a pervert and never talk to me again. It's just not expected from someone like me. I have grown up in a very stable and loving home with both my parents, whom I respect more than anyone. I am also an A-student and very involved in my youth group. I feel like I have no one to turn to for help and I keep moving further and further from Christ. I no longer can hear His whisper or even remember when I could. How can I stop this and become a godly woman?

So what can we learn from Heather, Denise, and Emily?

- Masturbation's not just a problem that guys may struggle with. It tempts most of us at some point in our lives, both males and females. No matter how "good" you are, smart you are, popular you are, or successful your parents are, you are susceptible to this temptation. No matter where you live, where you go to school, where you attend church, or where you hang out, you can be tempted to masturbate. Nothing makes you exempt.

- If you feel tempted to masturbate, it doesn't mean that you are a bad person, only that you are a human being with sexual desires and passions, as all of us are. If you've not been tempted in this way yet, there's certainly nothing wrong with you. Simply praise God and be determined to resist this temptation if it ever sneaks up on you.

- Masturbation can be habit-forming and addictive. People who are compulsive about masturbating find that even though they want to stop, they can't. The habit often controls them.

- The momentary relief that self-gratification may provide is not worth the long-term stress it can create. It can lead to shame, low self-esteem, and fear of what others might think or that something is wrong with you.

- Masturbation does not satisfy sexual desires; it intensifies them. If you give in to your sexual desires through masturbation, you do not gain practice in exercising self-control. What hope will you have when some smooth-talking guy starts whispering sweet nothings into your ear if you can't even control your desires when alone?

- Self-gratification can build what feels like a wall between God and you, causing you to lose the sense of His presence. Although God never leaves us, habitual sin causes us to feel distanced from Him and from the ones we love.
- You will not automatically stop masturbating once you get married. The habits you have as a single woman are the habits you will drag into your marriage.

Please understand that once you awaken your sexual desires, which masturbation does, you will find them very difficult to put back to sleep. Once you begin feeding baby monsters, their appetites grow bigger and they want MORE! It's better not to feed such a monster in the first place.

VICTORY IS POSSIBLE

While it's true that habitual masturbation is difficult to control, it's *not* impossible to control. As Crystal can testify, the only way to kill a bad habit is to starve it to death. Ever since she was a little girl, she'd been in the habit of masturbating herself to sleep most nights, but not anymore.

At first I masturbated just for the enjoyment of it, because it felt good. As a teenager, I came to believe that masturbation would relieve my stress so I could relax and go to sleep. I had no idea that I was creating a habit that would haunt me into my twenties.

When I began to understand what an addiction this was for me, I realized that God doesn't want me living in bondage to this sin. I've gone to bed in my dorm room, desperate to avoid masturbating because I've hated myself for feeling the need for it. I've been staying up at night, walking up and down the dormitory hallway until the wee hours of the morning in order to exhaust myself to the point that I can fall asleep without masturbating. It really did help to break my habit! After weeks of this, I can honestly say that I know I don't have to give in to this temptation any longer. God has shown me a way out.

FUELING YOUR OWN SEXUAL FIRE   47

Starving a bad habit can be painful, but it is not as painful as letting it rule over you. This is why Peter warned, "Dear friends, I urge you, as aliens and strangers in the world, to abstain from sinful desires, which war against your soul" (1 Peter 2:11).

THE WAY OF THE WORLD VS. THE WAY OF THE WORD

Unfortunately, we live in a world that endorses masturbation as an appropriate way to release sexual tension or desire. For example, Meghan Bainum, a University of Kansas school newspaper columnist (oh, and *Playboy* model), wrote:

> Sometimes, even if a partner is readily available for you to play around with, there's nothing like taking matters into your own hands.... But what happens when your erotic adventure is stifled by an unwelcome companion, such as a roommate? Masturbating in a group-living situation does pose some problems, but where there is a will, there is a way.[1]

While some well-meaning Christians disagree with our view, we strongly believe that masturbation can lead you away from God's perfect plan for your sexuality. Before you seek the advice of your peers or anyone else, seek His opinion through Scripture reading and prayer.

Here are some of the most common arguments you'll hear in favor of masturbation, along with our responses:

- *Sexual self-exploration is normal, healthy, and innocent.* While it may be normal and healthy for young children to "discover" their sexual organs and their response to genital stimulus, we believe there comes an age of accountability (sometime during puberty or soon thereafter) when everyone must learn sexual responsibility and self-control. When self-exploration becomes masturbation (which for females often involves sexual fantasies about others and sometimes the use of pornography), it becomes an unhealthy habit that strips a young person of sexual innocence.

We also believe that masturbation is not healthy because it can train a person to "fly solo," to operate independently of anyone else. When you masturbate, you train your body as well as your mind what to find pleasurable and how to orgasm.* When you marry, if your husband isn't able to please you in the exact same way, this could make your marital sex life very frustrating and disappointing. Just ask Quinn:

I was disappointed in our sex life when I got married. I expected that my husband would have the same magic touch that I had with myself, but he is rougher and more aggressive than I am used to. I've tried to teach him what I like, but one night after I tried to coach him, he responded, "Why don't you just do it yourself if you don't like the way I do it?" On the one hand, I was relived that I could finally do what felt good to me, but on the other hand, I know it must be a blow to his ego that I'm not as aroused by his touch as I am by my own.

Most husbands find pleasure and satisfaction in bringing their wives to orgasm. If you regularly find sexual release through masturbation, you may rob your future husband of this pleasure by feeling the need to "help him."

- *It doesn't involve anyone else, so it can't be wrong.* While masturbation may not involve someone else physically, it usually involves someone else mentally. To have an orgasm, the single woman typically entertains fantasies of people she is not married to when she masturbates. These mental fantasies are just as harmful to your sexual integrity as engaging in sexual activity with a partner, because you can create a standard in your mind that no human being, including your future husband, can live up to.

- *Scripture doesn't even mention it.* While the word *masturbation* isn't in Scripture, the Bible does address the related issues of lustful thoughts and sexual immorality in multiple places. Here are a few examples of what we believe the Bible says about masturbation and its related mental activities:

---

* *orgasm*—the climax of sexual excitement for a woman

But among you there must not be even a hint of sexual immorality, or of any kind of impurity, or of greed, because these are improper for God's holy people. (Ephesians 5:3)

Put to death, therefore, whatever belongs to your earthly nature: sexual immorality, impurity, lust, evil desires and greed, which is idolatry. Because of these, the wrath of God is coming. (Colossians 3:5)

It is God's will that you should be sanctified: that you should avoid sexual immorality; that each of you should learn to control [her] own body in a way that is holy and honorable, not in passionate lust like the heathen, who do not know God. (1 Thessalonians 4:3-5)

We are not prudes, and we know that almost everyone experiments with masturbation. But that doesn't mean it's good for you. Even if we bought into the argument that masturbation is not a sin because it isn't mentioned in Scripture, we would refer back to what Paul wrote in 1 Corinthians 10:23: "'Everything is permissible'—but not everything is beneficial. 'Everything is permissible'—but not everything is constructive."

The bottom line is that masturbation can enslave you and bring you into bondage. We believe that fact alone is enough reason to abstain from the practice altogether. If you have discovered the pleasure of masturbation, it is time to loosen its grip on you.

GIVING OUR DESIRES BACK TO GOD

We want to close this chapter with one final reason why masturbation is wrong: Self-gratification is a prideful response to our human desires. Such actions tell God, "You may want me to learn to wait to gratify my sexual desires until marriage, but I don't want to. Your way takes too long and requires too much self-control. I'm going to take care of things my way." Do you hear the pride in that attitude? Do you sense the rejection of God's sovereignty and ability to help you exercise self-control?

God made every fiber and every nerve of your body, and He knows how you feel. God knows you better than you know yourself. He knows that waiting is hard, but He also knows that His way is best.

Place your sexual desires back into God's hands rather than taking matters into your own. God gave you these desires in the first place, and He longs to help you control them until they can be fulfilled according to His plan. Once you allow Him to prove Himself in this area, you will understand that self-gratification isn't truly satisfying at all. If you want your body, mind, heart, and spirit to remain pure, strive for God-gratification instead of self-gratification.

Who may ascend the hill of the LORD? Who may stand in his holy place?
[She] who has clean hands and a pure heart, who does not lift up [her]
soul to an idol or swear by what is false.

Psalm 24:3-4

making friends with the mirror

And we, who with unveiled faces all reflect the Lord's glory, are being transformed into his likeness with ever-increasing glory.

2 CORINTHIANS 3:18

When you look into the mirror, what do you see? A friend or a foe? Are you thankful for God's creation or critical of His handiwork? How much time and energy do you spend critiquing and criticizing your facial features? your hair? your body? Do you compare yourself to magazine cover models or to your girlfriends, getting discouraged that you don't seem to measure up to everyone else?

What you see in the mirror has a lot to do with what you feel in your heart.

Perhaps you look into the mirror often because you *do* like what you see—a lot. Maybe you believe that others don't measure up to you. Perhaps vanity and pride are more of an issue for you than a poor body image.

We certainly hope that neither of these scenarios describes you. We hope you like what you see in the mirror because you are one of God's beautiful creations, but we also hope that you don't let your beauty go to your head. Somewhere in between "I hate the way I look!" and "Look at me! Aren't I hot?" lies a delicate balance that we pray you will find and maintain throughout life. Why is this so important? Because either extreme can lead you down the path of sexual compromise at lightning speed.

Looking back over my own life, I see how these extremes often drove me to look for love in all the wrong places. As I was going through puberty in my preteen years, I felt like a walrus—very chunky and awkward. I wondered why I couldn't be more petite like the cheerleaders at my school. However, by the time I was a freshman in high school, my body had totally changed. I had grown several inches taller and those extra few pounds seemed to settle in just the right places to give me some flattering curves. I liked the attention my new body got me, especially from older guys, and I learned that the more I could show off those curves with just the right clothes, the more attention I got. Sadly, my bold, new confidence led me into relationships with guys who had just as much appreciation for my body, but far less respect, and I became sexually active. I used my body to get their attention, and I felt I had to use my body to keep that attention.

Fast forward four years… I graduated from high school and went into the Air Force to earn money for college. In my first week of basic training, I had to weigh in and was devastated to be placed on the "chunky chicken list" until I lost ten pounds. I didn't like being told I was fat, and I desperately wanted affirmation that I was *not* too fat. Although I had committed to remaining sexually abstinent months before entering the Air Force, I suddenly found myself scanning the male recruits, hoping someone might be looking my way. I wondered if I was still sexually desirable, even as a "chunky chicken." During those few weeks of basic training, I entertained the sexual advances of three different young men, not because I wanted to have sex again, but because I needed affirmation that I was still beautiful, even with the extra weight.

While I'm not proud of my past, I'm telling you these intimate details because I want you to understand a very important principle: Whether it is an overly developed sense of pride in your appearance or the opposite, *either extreme can be hazardous to your sexual health.* If your vanity leads you into sexual situations with young men who think you look hot or if your poor body image causes you to latch on to any guy willing to affirm your sex appeal in spite of how you feel about yourself, you are compromising.

Far better to redefine beauty according to our Creator's definition rather than to look to the world and adopt its twisted definition.

Painting a New Picture of Perfect Beauty

Where does our society get its ideas about what makes a girl beautiful? Sharon Hersh, author of *"Mom, I Feel Fat!"* sat down with twenty-five middle-school-aged girls and asked them to describe the perfect girl. Their responses, in order of importance, were as follows:

- thin
- blond
- popular
- beautiful
- athletic
- has big breasts
- has a boyfriend
- confident
- straight white teeth (no braces!)
- has her own car
- doesn't have zits
- has her own phone[1]

We agree with Sharon—the only one we know who fits that description is Barbie. It's amazing how a childhood toy can mold a young girl's ideas about where beauty comes from. Nineteen-year-old Kim echoed the heart's cry of many young women when she told us:

> As I grew up, the reflection in my mirror looked increasingly more like my mom than Barbie. I felt so betrayed by my own body because it didn't grow into the shape I thought it should be.

Like Kim, many young women grow up with unrealistic expectations about their bodies. It's not just Barbie dolls that create these false ideas of beauty. So do television celebrities, movie stars, magazine cover models, fashion designers, and many other aspects of today's pop culture.

But where does beauty really come from? Let's go back to the Bible to see what the Creator of beauty has to say about where it comes from and how we are to use it.

> Charm is deceptive, and beauty is fleeting,
>   but a woman who fears [respects and serves] the LORD is to be praised.
>   (Proverbs 31:30)

Your beauty should not come from outward adornment, such as braided hair and the wearing of gold jewelry and fine clothes. Instead, it should be that of your inner self, the unfading beauty of a gentle and quiet spirit, which is of great worth in God's sight. For this is the way the holy women of the past who put their hope in God used to make themselves beautiful. (1 Peter 3:3-5)

Do these scriptures say that we shouldn't style our hair or wear nice jewelry or clothes? Of course not. The Bible simply says that this kind of beauty fades and can't be depended upon. These verses are good reminders that physical beauty isn't going to last forever and that our primary focus shouldn't be on outward beauty. However, the beauty that comes from loving and serving God with a happy heart is a beauty that endures even when your figure has fallen south and wrinkles adorn your face. True beauty doesn't come from fresh makeup, the latest hairstyle, or how you look in your blue jeans. Rather, it radiates from the inside out, from a heart that delights in the Lord.

Here's another verse to consider:

You became very beautiful and rose to be a queen. And your fame spread among the nations on account of your beauty, because the splendor I had given you made your beauty perfect, declares the Sovereign LORD. But you trusted in your beauty and used your fame to become a prostitute. You lavished your favors on anyone who passed by and your beauty became his. (Ezekiel 16:13-15)

The prophet Ezekiel was referring to Jerusalem in this passage and used this analogy to say, "Hey! You've taken the spiritual beauty that God gave you and served other gods with it! You're doing whatever you want to do instead of being an example to other nations!" We believe this passage also has a message for you today. God says (through Ezekiel), "The splendor I had given you made your beauty perfect." In other words, perfect beauty comes as a gift from the Lord to all who believe in Him, not from flawless skin, bleached teeth, or size zero jeans. God still bestows beauty on us—spiritual and physical beauty—so that we can bring glory and attention to Him as our Creator, not to ourselves. We are to trust in Him for the things we want (such as attention and affection in healthy relationships), not in our physical beauty. Such will eventually fail us, but God never will.

When we forget that beauty comes from a heart that loves God, we assume that beauty comes from a body that looks a certain way. What if your body doesn't look like the image of beauty that you have in your mind? What effect can that have on your self-image and your relationships? Perhaps Hannah can answer that question better than we can.

BEAUTY IN THE EYES OF A BOYFRIEND

Because nineteen-year-old Hannah is overweight, she says she doesn't feel beautiful at all. But being Mitch's girlfriend helps her cope with those feelings and gives her a sense of hope that if someone else finds her pretty enough to date, then maybe she's not so bad after all. Hannah assumed that having a boyfriend could medicate the pain of her poor self-image, but experience proved her wrong. She told us:

> Mitch and I have been dating for almost a year. At first he was charming and treated me well, but the magical moments have become a memory. It began with an occasional remark about how if I loved him, I'd be willing to have sex with him. Of course I loved him and desperately wanted him to love me back, so we began having sex. Then he wanted me to help him pay his bills, since he was in college and I was working. Again, I went along with it to prove my love and ensure that I wouldn't lose his. Then he began to say mean things about my looks such as, "If you want to be seen with me you've got to fix yourself up a little… Lay off the groceries—I don't want my friends to see me with a fat girl… If you can't doll yourself up better, I'm going to have to find another main squeeze." I guess I let him treat me this way because I'm afraid no one else would want to be with me since I'm overweight. If this is the price I have to pay for love, then I guess I'm willing to pay it, because I don't think I can live without him.

When we asked Hannah why she didn't think she could live without Mitch, she said that she wants the security of having a boyfriend, even if he treats her poorly.

But if she weren't so insecure, would she feel the same way? If she knew how precious and beautiful she is because she is the Lord's handiwork, would she need to have a boyfriend to feel lovable? Would she allow herself to be mistreated if she had a better self-image? Probably not.

Of course, as we said earlier, having a poor self-image isn't the only motivation for why a young woman engages in a sexual relationship. Sometimes the opposite is true.

WHEN BEAUTY LEADS YOU DOWN AN UGLY ROAD

Retta has won many beauty pageants, but winning the battle against her eating disorder and against sexual compromise proved far more difficult. She struggled for years with anorexia nervosa, an eating disorder characterized by a refusal to maintain adequate body weight and an intense fear of gaining weight or becoming fat, even though underweight. She says this:

> Growing up in the beauty pageant scene, I put a lot of pressure on myself to be thin and look beautiful. I starved myself to lose more and more weight, but no number on the scale ever seemed low enough for me. I found my identity in being skinny, and I feared what would happen if I ever started gaining weight.
>
> My eating disorder gave me a sense of power and control, as did my ability to attract a guy's attention with my looks. I started dating a Christian named Josh who treated me very respectfully, never putting any kind of pressure on me to get physical at all. I went up to a mountain retreat with some friends and called him to come up and join us. I had my own room, and when he agreed to drive up, I remember plotting that I was going to "reward" Josh for coming to see me. It was our six-month anniversary, and I was at my all-time lowest weight, which made me feel not just slender but also powerfully seductive. I decided I was going to give him my virginity that night, not realizing that I was robbing him of his in the process. I can't believe that feeling so beautiful led me to do such an ugly thing.

As Retta's story illustrates, being thin may make you feel attractive on the outside, but if you are using your beauty in a selfish way, you are an unattractive person on the inside—where it counts the most. You can, however, choose inward *and* outward beauty.

CHOOSING TO BE BEAUTIFUL

We thought about inserting a graph or chart in this chapter to show minimum and maximum weights for young women, but decided against it. Why? Because we don't want to perpetuate the myth that your beauty comes from a particular number on your bathroom scale. Yet, even though true beauty cannot be measured by outward appearances, looking good on the outside is relatively important because you represent God. The secret to looking and feeling your personal best is eating healthy foods and exercising your body. As you simply eat the right foods in the right amounts and exercise to enhance or maintain your metabolism and muscle strength, your body will settle into a weight that is absolutely perfect for you.

But your beauty is not "on hold" until you reach a perfect weight. You can feel beautiful at any weight, or you can be miserable until your scale reads some magical number that you may never reach or be satisfied with. The choice is yours.

Think about it. You probably know someone who looks great in her blue jeans but has such a self-centered personality or rotten attitude that "beautiful" would never be one of the words you'd use to describe her. On the other hand, you probably know a girl who may not have modeling agents beating down her door yet is one of the most beautiful people you know.

One of the most beautiful young women we know is twenty-year-old Tracy.

PAMPERING WITH A PURPOSE

At five feet ten inches with a size sixteen frame, Tracy's beauty surpasses any teeny-tiny, wafer-thin model we've ever seen. She is too smart to subscribe to the myth that a flat stomach will equate to a lifetime of happiness, nor does she put too much stock in her outward appearance (although she is a very pretty woman). You'll never hear Tracy complain about the size of her thighs or even the massive scar on her chest from the heart surgery she had as a child. Her beauty radiates from the inside out, and she reflects the incomparable beauty of Jesus Christ like no young woman we've ever known. Her positive attitude, servant's heart, and deep desire to help others make her absolutely stunning.

While Tracy's ultimate career goal is to become a cosmetologist with her own salon, she longs to help other women discover and enhance their natural beauty in order to feel good about who God made them to be, specializing in not just physical but also *spiritual* makeovers. Because of this, she ministers to female hospital patients by washing and styling their hair, doing their nails, and making them feel better about themselves while restricted to a hospital bed. Now that's pampering with a purpose!

Tracy has discovered that true beauty radiates from within and ultimately brings glory to God because it draws others to want to know Him as they get to know us better. By loving and serving Christ wholeheartedly, you can, like Tracy, discover the true source of genuine beauty.

Another beautiful girl we know is Tina. Once tormented by the reflection in her mirror, she is a living proof that you can believe you are beautiful when you choose to believe what your Creator says about you.

COMPLIMENTED BY THE CREATOR

Growing up, Tina developed a severe case of acne that left deep scars not just on her face but on her soul as well. Peers had teased and taunted her mercilessly, and she believed that she was ugly. It wasn't until she attended a youth retreat as an eighteen-year-old that Tina began to heal and change the way she viewed herself. Several weeks after the retreat, she wrote the following note:

> Song of Songs 4:7 says, "All beautiful you are, my darling; there is no flaw in you." God thinks I'm beautiful! The Creator of the Universe who hung the sun, moon, and stars calls me beautiful! I never realized how powerful those words are. If God spoke and the world was created, then His word is power. If God said, "Let there be light," and there was, then if He says I'm beautiful,

I am. It may take me a while to see myself this way, but God said it and that makes it true. If God thinks I'm beautiful, then I guess what other people think doesn't really matter.

In this day of plastic surgery, liposuction, and "extreme" makeovers, we think it's time all young women see themselves as God sees them, just as Tina has. Embrace these words from Psalm 139:13-16:

> For you created my inmost being;
>> You knit me together in my mother's womb.
> I praise you because I am fearfully and wonderfully made;
>> your works are wonderful,
>> I know that full well.
> My frame was not hidden from you
>> when I was made in the secret place.
> When I was woven together in the depths of the earth,
>> your eyes saw my unformed body.
> All the days ordained for me
>> were written in your book
>> before one of them came to be.

As we close this chapter on body image, we would like you to think about the women you respect and admire. Consider female Bible characters, historical figures, or special ladies in your own life and make a list of those who impress you the most. Then allow us to ask you the following questions.

WHAT WILL HISTORY REFLECT ABOUT YOU?

Why are the women you listed so special? What did each of them contribute to society or to your life? Do you admire them for their physical beauty or their weight or because of the beauty of their deeds and the value of the investments they've made in other people's lives?

What about you? What do you want to be remembered for? Your obsession with your own appearance and weight or your passion to love and serve others? Do you want to spend your life looking into mirrors, distracted by your own reflection and how your looks compare to others, or do you want to invest your life looking beyond yourself and into a world of people who need to experience the love of God through you?

Remember, Jesus said we are to love others *as we love ourselves* (see Matthew 22:39). Therefore, to truly love others the way God wants us to, we must start with the person we see looking back at us in the mirror each morning. Shoot for that perfect balance somewhere between the extremes of hatred and vanity. Adopt an attitude that says, "I love myself because God made me, and I'm growing more beautiful by the day because I'm becoming more like Jesus."

By making friends with the mirror and moving on to more important concerns, you'll reflect a much deeper beauty than any movie star or model, and you will discover a purpose to your life that brings much greater joy than some magic number on the scale.

 The king is enthralled by your beauty; honor him, for he is your lord....
All glorious is the princess within her chamber; her gown is interwoven
with gold. In embroidered garments she is led to the king; her virgin
companions follow her and are brought to you. They are led in with joy
and gladness; they enter the palace of the king.

Psalm 45:11,13-15

doing a reality check

We have renounced secret and shameful ways; we do not use deception, nor do we distort the word of God. On the contrary, by setting forth the truth plainly we commend ourselves to every man's conscience in the sight of God.

2 CORINTHIANS 4:2

In the May 22, 2002, issue of the *New York Times,* reporter Corey Kilgannon wrote:

> By day, she was Christina Long, a thirteen-year-old altar girl and a co-captain of the cheerleading team at St. Peter Roman Catholic School in Danbury, Conn., where the principal said she was "a good student and well behaved."
>
> But in the evenings, the authorities say, she logged onto the Internet using the screen name LongToohot4u and the slogan, "I will do anything at least once." In her bedroom, the police say, she used her computer to troll chat rooms and meet adult men for sex, her marital status listed as, "i might be single i might not be."
>
> Early Monday, Christina's body was found in a steep ravine off a county road in Greenwich. She had been strangled, the authorities say, by a twenty-five-year-old Greenwich man she had met in one of those chat rooms.
>
> The man, Saul Dos Reis, had had several sexual encounters with Christina, the authorities say, before killing her Friday night and dumping her body.[1]

If you're thinking, *That will never happen to me!* think again. Why *not* you? In fact, if you choose to interact with strangers on the Internet, what makes you exempt from such entanglements? How do you know that the seemingly nice people at the other computer terminals are really interested in your well-being? How do you know they are who they say they are? What gives you enough confidence in their character to give them one ounce of your attention, let alone a significant investment of your time and emotional energies? Can you be sure they aren't actually mass murderers, serial rapists, or child pornographers?

NOT THE REAL THING

While meeting guys over the Internet may seem like safe excitement, don't be fooled. Cyber relationships can be as far from real life as the fairy tales you read as a child. It may sound wonderful to be Cinderella or Snow White and fall in love with a handsome prince, marry, and live "happily ever after," but that's not how relationships work in real life, and for good reason.

How much did Cinderella and Snow White know about their princes when they agreed to marry them—besides the fact that they were handsome and charming? Zero. Zilch. Zip. Nada. While you may have thought this sounded wonderful as a little girl, we hope you are wise enough and mature enough to see that such tales are based in fantasy, and many fantasies, if actually lived out, have the makings of a tragedy rather than a grand love story.

We don't have to tell you how popular Internet chat rooms are. You likely know, because even if you have never surfed the Net to meet someone, it's likely you know someone who has. Or perhaps you or someone you know has even gone so far as engaging in cybersex, where two people turn each other on with sexual conversations over the Internet.

John Eldredge wrote of this new fascination with cyberspace in his book *The Journey of Desire:*

> Cyber relationships have launched the search for the golden man or woman
> to a new level because the mystique can be maintained much longer. Internet
> love doesn't ever have bad breath, you don't get an STD from a terminal, and
> no one ever has to know.[2]

John is right. In an Internet relationship you only see the good things the other person wants you to see through e-mails and instant messages. In real relationships with real people, you see the whole package—the good, the bad, *and* the ugly.

Internet relationships can be misleading and harmful to your ability to form healthy relationships with guys you interact with in person. It is hard for any real relationship to live up to the fantasy of a virtual relationship. In reality, even healthy relationships are at times disappointing, frustrating, and boring. So if a virtual relationship actually develops into a real one, that mystique will wear off and the disappointments, frustrations, and boredom of real relationships will eventually surface.

Also, in virtual relationships you get only a one-dimensional view of someone's character. You see only the side that the person allows you to see. However, in real relationships, you get a more complex, three-dimensional view as you watch how a guy interacts with his parents, how he treats his little sister, how he treats his friends as well as other girls, and so on. You need to see all of these things before you can make a fair judgment about a person's true character and whether he is appealing to you or not.

Figure 7.1 sums up the differences between virtual relationships and the real thing.

WHAT'S THE APPEAL?

Why look for romance on the Web? What makes these virtual relationships so alluring?

VIRTUAL RELATIONSHIPS	REAL RELATIONSHIPS
• based on fantasy	• built on reality
• require little effort	• require relational work
• involve no accountability	• lived out in the presence of others
• involve false mystique and pretense	• require integrity and mutual trust
• give a one-dimensional view of the person	• give a three-dimensional view of the person

Figure 7.1

Here are some of the reasons we've heard, along with our responses, and what we believe are the real, but perhaps subconscious, reasons.

- *It is exciting to be intimate with a stranger.* While we agree that new relationships can be exciting, don't kid yourself. Since when is sitting at a desk and typing back and forth "intimate"? Learning new things about a person you just met is *not* intimacy, it's just new. Intimacy is seeing what is *truly* on the inside of a person, which can only be discovered face to face, over long periods of time. When you first meet a guy and spend hours talking with him, it feels exciting and stimulating. But be careful not to mistake *intensity* for *intimacy.* Intensity fades as the newness wears off, but intimacy continues to blossom the longer you know a person.

- *I can be anyone I want to be while online.* This response reflects poor self-esteem. Because you are afraid people won't be interested in the real you, you like pretending to be someone you perceive as more attractive or fun than you are. But if you aren't yourself, if you hide the real you or pretend to be someone else, how can you feel good about this guy's feelings for you? He doesn't even know you. And remember that *he* can also pretend to be anybody he wants to be.

- *I appreciate someone being interested in getting to know me, regardless of what I look like.* But don't think for a minute that he's not eventually going to be very interested in what you look like. That's just the way guys are wired. Then what will you do? Why go there? Don't get hooked.

- *I enjoy just conversing with a guy without having the expectation placed on me to get physical.* You may not want to get physical with him now, but after you've poured out your heart to him and swallowed every line he's fed you, you are going to want to move beyond the emotional. Once you give him your heart, then the urge to meet him, be in his arms, feel his kiss, and so on can quickly lure you down the road toward sexual compromise.

We suspect that in addition to *low self-esteem,* young women desire to meet people over the Internet because of these two issues:

- *Loneliness.* If you don't feel you have any close personal friends or any prospects for a boyfriend, you might be tempted to look beyond your part of the world into the bigger World Wide Web for friendship. But because Internet relationships often use up the energy that would normally be invested in real relationships, you may be poking holes in the very bucket you are trying to fill and losing out on chances to develop more meaningful friendships.

- *Peer pressure.* Just because "everyone is doing it" doesn't mean it's a good idea, nor does it mean that it's okay or safe. If your friends are meeting guys on the Web, you might want to loan them this book and encourage them to read this chapter in particular. Rather than letting them pull you down the wrong path, encourage them to find the right path to healthy relationships.

LESSONS LEARNED

Of course we can't say that all cyberspace encounters end badly, but virtual relationships are far more likely to be misleading than real ones. While writing this book, we asked 120 young women if they had ever been lured into an unhealthy relationship on the Internet, and to tell us about their experience. We were hoping to get at least four or five responses. We were shocked to receive ten times that amount. While we couldn't include all the responses we received, Amber, Aime, and Tiffany's responses represent what many of your peers told us about their experiences of surfing the Net to meet a guy.

When Amber was thirteen she became depressed but found the Internet to be a welcome escape. She told us, "I discovered that I could make up my own identity and no one knew about my past or cared how I looked." Amber began to spend so much time meeting guys on the Internet that her parents expressed concern about what she was doing on the computer for so long. She lied about what she was doing and started going online when her parents wouldn't know. She had this to say:

> One Saturday while my parents were away I spent eight hours straight on the Internet! I continually met more and more people and talked on the phone

with some of them as well. Over time, real people became less appealing to me and all I wanted to do was talk to my Internet friends. They seemed much more interesting to me and pretending to be someone else was more exciting than being myself.

I got so involved with this one guy I met on the Internet that we decided to become boyfriend and girlfriend. I went to visit my cousins in California and since he lived nearby, we decided to meet each other. We set up a time and a place, and my cousin and I just waited and waited. He never showed up. I think this was probably the grace of God, since he could have been a murderer or rapist. I really had no way of knowing anything about his character.

Amber now recognizes just how dangerous a game she was playing by pretending to be someone she wasn't and by agreeing to meet a stranger in person. She says that the toll these fantasy relationships took on her real ones wasn't worth the price she paid and the time that she wasted.

Aime met Zach in a Christian singles chat room. At first he appeared to be a friendly guy who was honestly seeking God. But eventually reality brought the fantasy to a somewhat sobering end. Aime admitted:

Zach and I soon began talking over Instant Messenger more and more, until we would be on the computer together for hours at a time. After a few weeks, he decided to come visit me. When I saw him, he didn't strike me as someone I would have been attracted to at all if I had just met him on the street. But since he'd come to visit me, I took him around town and to church. I kept thinking, *Why is he here? I'm only eighteen and I'm not ready for this serious of a relationship!* In spite of these red flags and even warnings from some friends and family, I got physical with him and went way too far. I admit that I was feeling lonely, and it was nice to have someone pay attention to me. We didn't have intercourse, but we came close, and that really scared me to think that I almost had sex with someone that I didn't think I even wanted to be with once I met him.

Aime has decided to stick with real relationships from here on out so that she never falls into the fantasy trap like that again.

Tiffany invested two years in an Internet relationship with Wes before she recognized that this virtual relationship wasn't blossoming into the intimate friendship she wanted. Because she spent most of her free time on the computer interacting with him instead of spending time with her family and friends, those relationships weren't growing either. Tiffany confesses:

> Wes gave me tons of compliments, and it was so good to hear that kind of stuff from a guy, especially when my dad was complaining about my attitude and how crabby I was getting. Wes never complained about my attitude because he never saw me act this way. I started losing friends because I was spending all my time on the Internet with him instead of with them. My grades started suffering because I wasn't studying.
>
> After several months I was afraid Wes would start losing interest in me, because he began talking about other girls he had met. I started making things up about places I had gone and things I had done to sound more exciting, thinking that would keep him interested in me. The relationship eventually died out when he decided he wanted a "real" girlfriend.
>
> When it was over with, I was pretty devastated, because I was truly convinced that we were going to marry. I had a broken heart, some bad family relationships that took over a year to rebuild, and no strong friendships, because I'd ignored all my friends while I was so involved with Wes.

Perhaps you can relate to Amber, Aime, and Tiffany because of your own experiences surfing the Net to meet a guy. If so, we'd like to help you.

GET UNTANGLED FROM THE WEB

If you have already invested in unhealthy virtual relationships or are currently doing so, we have a few tips for how you can get untangled from the World Wide Web.

- *Avoid private, personal e-mail accounts that no one else knows about or has access to.* You may not think that anyone else has a right to know about your cyberactivities or communications, but where there are no secrets, there are no lies. Don't give in to the temptation of creating a double life for yourself like Christina did (the girl mentioned earlier, found murdered by her cybersex partner). She paid too high a price for those secrets in the long run.

- *Avoid cyberconversations with anyone you have never met face to face.* Stick to real relationships with real people so you can see the bigger picture of who those people really are and how they interact with others.

- *Hit the Ignore button if a previous cyberbuddy continues to invade your space using Instant Messenger or e-mail.* Remember, you are under no obligation to respond. He'll eventually get the hint or lose interest altogether. You're not being rude, but merely protecting yourself.

EMBRACING REAL INTIMACY

You may have heard some people say that fantasy relationships are much better than real ones, but is this true? Not by a long shot. Perhaps people who pursue virtual relationships have never tasted how good reality can be. When someone knows you inside and out, knows all your little quirks and annoying habits, knows everything about you there is to know, and yet is absolutely crazy about you, it's an awesome thing. Such genuine intimacy enhances your self-esteem, your life, and your happiness.

You know what else? There's Someone who already knows you that well and loves you that much. He knew you before you were even born. He knew what every day of your entire life would hold. He knew about every mistake you'd ever make, every rebellious thought you'd ever have, and every sin you'd ever commit, yet He loves you so much that He chose to die for you. Because Christ's death on the cross paid the penalty for all of your sin, not only can you never be separated from God, but you also can have access to Him through the Holy Spirit any time of day or night. You don't have to wait until He signs on to His computer to get a message to Him. You don't have to keep checking e-mails to see if He sent you a message—there are plenty awaiting you in the Bible. Through prayer, you have unlimited, 24/7 instant messaging with God. So when you long for intimacy and connection, don't get virtual…*get real!*

> *I pray that out of his glorious riches he may strengthen you with power through his Spirit in your inner being, so that Christ may dwell in your hearts through faith. And I pray that you, being rooted and established in love, may have power, together with all the saints, to grasp how wide and long and high and deep is the love of Christ, and to know this love that surpasses knowledge—that you may be filled to the measure of all the fullness of God.*
>
> *Ephesians 3:16-19*

breaking the cycle of abuse

> For our struggle is not against flesh and blood, but against the rulers, against the authorities, against the powers of this dark world and against the spiritual forces of evil in the heavenly realms. Therefore put on the full armor of God, so that when the day of evil comes, you may be able to stand your ground.
>
> EPHESIANS 6:12-13

Have you ever shopped for a wedding gift? Maybe you've gone to several department stores and used their cool bridal registry computers that list everything the bride and groom would like to receive. It's fun to browse through a couple's selections to get an idea of their tastes, especially their choice of china, crystal, and silverware patterns. You can just imagine how beautifully these things will adorn their dining table when they entertain guests. Based on the china pattern that the bride and groom select, just one plate or cup or bowl can be over twenty-five dollars. A complete place setting of china can cost hundreds of dollars—and that's not counting the crystal stemware or silverware!

Now imagine this. What if after the wedding the couple uses their expensive china plates as dog and cat dishes, their crystal glasses as storage containers in the garage, and their new silverware as garden tools? Sound ridiculous? Absolutely.

But does the misuse of these expensive items make them any less valuable? Once retrieved and washed up, will they still adorn a tabletop with beauty and style? SURE. Even though they've been misused and abused, they can still be used for the valuable purposes for which they were created.

Sadly, many young women who are beautiful beyond description and valuable beyond measure have lost sight of just how precious they are and now view themselves as dirty or worthless because they have been used in a way that God never intended.

Of course, we are referring to young women who have been sexually abused, of which there are many. Consider these startling statistics:

- Approximately one in three girls will be sexually abused before the age of eighteen.[1]
- One study revealed that during a twenty year period, as many as twelve million women and children—nearly 10 percent of the current female population of the United States—had been raped.[2]
- One in four college women have been or will be the victim of rape or attempted rape.[3]

While rape and sexual abuse are absolute tragedies, the tragedy deepens if the abused person doesn't get help for coping with the rape or abuse. When the wounds of abuse go untreated, the abused person often becomes an abuser of others. The good news is that it does not have to be that way and treatment can help you avoid that vicious cycle.

As you read the following stories, note that abuse comes in many forms—physical, verbal, and sexual—and can come from a variety of relationships, such as strangers, boyfriends, employers, coworkers, friends, and relatives. Although the type of abuse may vary, all abusers are selfish people who use someone in ways that aren't consistent with how they deserve to be treated as a precious child of God.

SHELLY'S STORY

On April 7, 2000, a stranger forced his way into Shelly's apartment and violently raped her. She spent six days in the hospital after the rape, grateful to be alive. But before long, numbness set in:

> Within a period of months, I had no feeling, no concern for myself or for others. I began to look at men who resembled my attacker and found them attractive. I disregarded the morals and values I once took great pride in

keeping and began having sex with these men. In my mind I was regaining the power and control that I had lost in the rape. I was the one in charge. I could choose who and when and how I did it. I did not care for these men, I did not care for myself, and I never acknowledged or sought the One who had saved my life.

Eventually Shelly went to counseling and learned about sexual addiction. In time she realized she was using sex to numb her pain and regain a sense of control. While she knows she is not defined by her past, she says not a day goes by that she is not reminded of what happened. Thanks to her wise and courageous choice to talk with someone about her behavior and feelings, Shelly's starting to heal from the wounds of the abuse. She has also come to understand that God has forgiven her, loves her, and is with her always. Nothing changes that, not even rape or promiscuity!

Unfortunately, abuse isn't always the result of a stranger's offense. Sometimes the offense comes from someone you know, trust, and perhaps even love.

MEGAN'S STORY

When Megan was seventeen, she became interested in Bob. She was a Christian and had no intention of having sex before marriage. After seeing each other all summer, the two became serious, spending more and more time talking and kissing. Things took an unexpected turn one night when they went to a park for a picnic on a double date with friends and found themselves alone when the other couple wandered off.

We started out just kissing, but suddenly Bob got on top of me and then he raped me. It felt like I was in another world. I kept telling him to stop, but he ignored me. I didn't really comprehend what actually happened until I saw blood in my underwear later.

I remember feeling so confused. *Does this mean he really likes me?* If he had been a stranger, I would have fought him, but I trusted Bob. How could I have been so naive?

Within days, a few of my friends asked if it was true that Bob and I had had sex. I denied it to everyone. Any affection I had toward Bob turned to anger when I learned that he was bragging about the incident to others. I pictured myself walking into the locker room while he was bragging about what happened and saying, "Why don't you tell them the truth, Bob? It was rape and you know it!" I was so angry, and I hated him so much. I was so ashamed and embarrassed. I couldn't wait for my period to start so I'd know I wasn't pregnant.

After the rape I was very different. I became promiscuous* and got pregnant by another guy, only to have an abortion.† I became very dependent on guys and went from one relationship to another, dropping them whenever I got bored.

I am just so thankful that the Lord eventually showed me how to forgive Bob and move on without abusing *myself* any longer.

Megan began to understand that she could change when she saw a *700 Club* interview with someone who had been date raped. The woman talked about the freedom she experienced after forgiving her abuser. Megan wanted to be free from her anger and from her promiscuity, so she started praying about her bitterness. With the help of a counselor, she began to see that Bob was a lost, eighteen-year-old boy when he abused her. Megan was eventually able to forgive him and experienced freedom from her hatred toward him. She also began to see herself differently and felt lighter and more at peace.

MY OWN STORY

I can certainly sympathize with Megan because of the sexual abuse and date rape I experienced as a teen. As I entered puberty and blossomed physically, two uncles whom I loved and trusted began pursuing me without apology, flirting with me

---

* *promiscuous*—willing to have sex outside of a committed relationship

† *abortion*—terminating a pregnancy by having the unborn baby removed from the womb and disposed of

and luring me into compromising situations. Although fear kept me from giving in completely to their sexual advances, I loved the sense of power that flirting with them gave me. Both uncles told me that it was to be "our little secret," but they obviously talked about me between themselves. One later confessed to placing a bet as to which of them would "triumph" first at getting me in bed. Although neither succeeded, I began seeing myself as dirty.

I eventually drifted into the wrong place with the wrong person at the wrong time. When I was fourteen, I went behind my parents' back to be with an eighteen-year-old boy. When he date raped me, I never told anyone because of the fear of getting in trouble for inviting him over while no one else was at home. I had such low self-esteem and a high need for emotional connection that, believe it or not, I actually had hopes of cultivating a relationship with him, even after he raped me! But he had already gotten what he wanted, and I was left numb from the sting of both abuse and rejection.

When I began officially dating, I quickly caved in to sexual pressure. I put up little resistance to sexual advances whenever I thought it might lead to a romantic relationship. This vicious cycle went on for over five years until I woke up to the fact that I was allowing myself to be used and was using others in ways that God never intended.

SEVEN THINGS YOU NEED TO KNOW ABOUT ABUSE

We pray that you never experience any type of abuse, sexual or otherwise, but we also realize that many of you already have. If you are ever the victim of abuse or have been in the past, here are some valuable tips for helping you cope with such trauma and stop the cycle of abuse.

1. *Tell someone!* Don't suffer in silence. Whether you tell a parent, teacher, pastor, youth leader, professional counselor, teen-hotline operator, or another trusted adult, open up to someone who can help you process what has taken place and guide you down a pathway toward healing. If the person you tell doesn't believe you, tell someone else until you get some help. It is best that you tell someone immediately after being abused, especially in the case of rape so that evidence can be collected

and criminal charges filed. If you haven't talked to someone about it, even if it happened long ago, do so right away.

2. *Don't EVER tolerate someone's abuse—verbal, physical, or sexual.* If your boyfriend treats you poorly, keep in mind that you teach people how to treat you. If you tolerate the abuse, it enables him to think that it's okay for him to talk to you that way or to take advantage of you. If you are so desperate to have a boyfriend that you allow one to treat you like dirt, go back to chapter 4 and read Myth 3. Then kick that abusive boyfriend out to the curb before the next trash pick-up day, and expect the next one to treat you like the young woman of God that you truly are.

3. *Do not buy into the lie that you did something to deserve the abuse.* No one EVER deserves to be abused. Many women never press charges against a man who has sexually abused them because they feel as if they may have "brought it on themselves" by something they did or said. *No one deserves to be abused, regardless of how she dresses, where she goes, or what she does.* Read that sentence again, and believe it. Even if you initiate physical involvement, you have the right to change your mind and choose not to engage in further sexual activity at any point. Of course it's wise not to put yourself in compromising situations in the first place, but even if you do, it doesn't give another person the right to abuse you.

Here are some practical ways to avoid being sexually abused or raped:
1. Avoid being out alone after dark, if possible.
2. Lock the doors when you are home alone. If you are home alone frequently, don't advertise that fact to others.
3. When out on a date, stay in relatively public places where people could hear you if you screamed for help.
4. Don't engage in sexually arousing behaviors with your date, like inappropriate flirting, deep passionate kissing, or mutual masturbation.
5. Maintain firm boundaries. If someone attempts to get sexual with you, make it clear that you will not allow your boundary to be crossed. Speak up, pull away, or walk away altogether if necessary.

4. *It's okay to be angry at your abuser, but don't take that anger out on other people.* Many women who have been abused feel the urge to "punish" or "get even" with a date for abuse suffered at the hands of someone else. It is not uncommon for them to want to restage sexual situations so that they can regain the sense of control they lost when they were abused. Such dysfunctional behaviors show enormous disrespect of other men and abusing them will only serve to perpetuate your problems, not solve them.

5. *Rape and promiscuity are entirely different things.* If you have been raped, do not make the mistake of believing that you are no longer pure or that you have no reason to save yourself any longer. The status of your purity isn't determined by whether anyone has penetrated your genitals or physically forced you to do things you didn't want to do, but by whether you have chosen to use your body to sexually stimulate or grant sexual pleasure to another. If you have never made that kind of conscious, willing decision, but were raped or sexually abused, you are still pure.

6. *Make it your goal to forgive your abuser.* That may seem like the last thing in the world you'd want to do, but it will free you from bitterness. Hurting people hurt people, and most likely your abuser was also abused. That does not excuse the person or lessen your pain, but understanding the other person's motivation or past experiences can help you forgive. You never know what kind of pain drove your abuser to do the things he (or she) did or what kind of abuse that person suffered at the hands of someone else. Whether your abuser ever apologizes or even acknowledges the pain he caused, choosing to forgive him will free *you* from resentment and hatred, burdens too heavy for you to drag through life.

7. *While you'll never forget the abuse that was done to you, you can learn to cope responsibly with it and grow in spite of it.* Many victims of sexual abuse and rape go on to have very healthy marriages and productive lives, often reaching out to help others cope with the emotions that stem from abusive relationships. Sharing your recipe for survival can bring not only healing in the lives of others, but also great joy to your own life as you witness God's comfort flow to them through your words of compassion and encouragement.

YOUR HOPE FOR A BRIGHT FUTURE

Remember, you are a child of God, the bride of Christ, and a precious daughter of the King of the universe. Even if someone treats you less than royally or uses you for a purpose other than what God intended, *never forget who you really are.*

You deserve to be treated with dignity and respect. Period.

Also remember that others are worthy of the same respect. Don't allow the cycle of abuse to continue to destroy your life and your relationships. Draw a line in the sand and refuse to allow your future to be hindered by your past. God has great things in store for you as you seek to discover the true purpose for which you were created—a divine purpose, indeed!

"For I know the plans I have for you," declares the LORD, "plans to prosper you and not to harm you, plans to give you hope and a future."

Jeremiah 29:11

avoiding the destruction of others

pursuing power

I pray also that the eyes of your heart may be enlightened in order that you may know the hope to which he has called you, the riches of his glorious inheritance in the saints, and his incomparably great power for us who believe.

EPHESIANS 1:18-19

"Pick Him Up Tips"
"Make Your Ex-Boyfriend Want You Back"
"Get Him to Do Anything You Want."[1]

These are just a few of the many magazine headlines that scream for your attention. The media is constantly bombarding you with the message that if you want a guy, you've got the power to get him—so *use it!* Articles such as "30 Days to Girl Power" and "428 Ways to Be a Knockout, Dress to Thrill, [and] Get Him to Call Tonight!"[2] could lead a girl to wonder if there is something wrong with her if she is not trying to get a guy to give her attention and feed her ego.

We are living in an age when many women are using guys for their own self-satisfaction and are more predatory than their male counterparts. Many are desperate for affirmation that they are desirable and often control others in their pursuit of that affirmation. While it's appropriate and healthy for any female not to want to be overpowered by a male, it's not appropriate to strive for the reverse—*girls overpowering guys.*

Here are a few examples of the manipulation* games some young women play in their quest to gain a sense of power over young men:

---

* *manipulation*—attempting to control someone unfairly for your own personal satisfaction

- When Lisa gets dressed each morning, she considers what guys she will be seeing that day and dresses seductively to catch their eye so that they'll flirt with her. (Lisa is abusing her power by using her sex appeal and immodest attire to manipulate men into giving her the attention she wants.)

- Marissa finds that when a guy acts as if he's interested in her and goes out of his way to be around her, she quickly loses interest in him. However, if he plays hard to get, she can't get him out of her mind and attempts to reel him her direction by flirting. She thrives on the challenge of conquering a guy's resolve. (Marissa isn't as interested in a genuine, intimate relationship as she is in boosting her own ego by turning a guy's head and luring him in with her seductive power.)

- Kathy has little interest in Jason, who obviously thinks the world of her the way he showers her with compliments. However, she will go out with him if he offers to buy her dinner or if she just needs an ego boost. (Kathy is taking advantage of Jason's affection and his pocketbook, as she has no intention of ever reciprocating his feelings.)

Many girls no longer govern themselves by what is right (according to Scripture) but by what is popular, and girls overpowering guys has unfortunately become a popular pursuit. Perhaps you've thought, *If everybody else is doing it, so can I.* But let's remember what our mothers tell us—"If everybody else jumped off a building, would you do it?" Mom is right. Just because others are doing it, doesn't make it right or wise.

A BRAVE NEW BREED OR A BIG MISTAKE?

While writing an article for the *New York Times* called, "Girls Gone Macho,"[3] a reporter asked people how they felt about this new breed of seductive, power-hungry young women who boldly pursue boyfriends and take the lead in relationships. In the article, Tabi Upton, a counselor who sees between twenty and thirty teenagers each month, was quoted as saying, "The teenage boys I see often say the girls push them for sex and expect them to ask them for sex and will bring it up if boys don't ask. There has been a shift where girls now see themselves as sexualized and approach men with pretty much the attitude 'This is all I have to offer.'"

Lila Zimmerman, age sixteen, said the arrangement works out to be beneficial to the boys, because they don't have to put themselves at risk of rejection. "They don't have to be the embarrassed ones," she said. "I guess now it's our turn."

Upton also told of a fifteen-year-old girl who embraced the role of vixen as portrayed by pop culture. "She saw this stuff in the movies, on MTV, and she had sex with several guys." Upton went on to say that the girl got pregnant and was pretty sure it was by one of two guys. In addition, she contracted a sexually trans-mitted disease. In hindsight, the girl questioned, "Oh, why did I do this?" Upton concluded that the teenager was just hungry for love and wanted to look brave and adventurous. "It looks so exciting in the videos and so wonderful in the movies, but it isn't." The teen placed the baby for adoption.

Even if your pursuit of power doesn't land you in such a dilemma, it can cer-tainly cause you to lower your relational standards in an attempt to get a guy to do what you want. Carrie told us:

I decided I didn't need to sit back and wait around for a guy to come to me. If I wanted a guy, I could take the initiative and go after him. When I was seventeen, I met a guy at youth group who I thought was perfect for me because he was cute and a Christian. Though there was mutual attraction, he neglected to ask for my phone number. A friend and I decided to look him up in the phone book and give him a call. Forty people had the same last name! I hate to admit it, but we called every one until we found him.

Throughout that one-year relationship, I experienced many frustrations, hardships, and tears because I really wanted *him* to begin pursuing *me,* but the harder I tried to get him to take the lead and be romantic, the more he tended to take the "back seat" and let me be the "driver." I called him; I asked him out; I called all the shots. I drove us out on dates, I often paid for the entire night out, and I always initiated everything—including the physi-cal contacts. He didn't treat me the way I wanted to be treated, so I tried to *make* him. What a mistake!

It used to be that the only appropriate time for a girl to ask a guy out was for the Sadie Hawkins dance. Now young women not only track guys down and do the asking out, but they also initiate the physical relationship. In the past, if a girl gave in to sexual pressures, she felt victimized and used. More and more, young women are doing the victimizing and using.

We asked several guys how they feel about young women who pursue guys and take the lead in a relationship. Here's what they said:

Brent, age 16: The girls are way more aggressive than the boys and try too hard to have control over everything. It's scary.

Victor, age 17: When a girl comes after me, it makes me want to run. There was this girl who used to write me notes and put them in my locker almost every day. I never wrote her back, hoping she would take the hint, but then she started calling and even driving by my house. She just kept trying and trying to get me to play the game, but I wouldn't play. I guess she finally got tired of waiting, because she doesn't write or call anymore. But now I'm almost scared that when a girl starts showing a little bit of interest in me that she's going to start stalking me like that. I'd rather have a girlfriend who is going to let me lead in the relationship.

Chad, age 19: I just feel nowadays that my virginity means nothing.... There are so many girls tempting me to do wrong that I finally gave in one night and found myself an inch away from losing my physical virginity. I so want to save everything for marriage, everything—the hand holding, hugs, kisses— but I find myself dating the wrong type of girls and can't seem to stay away from them.

No respectable guy wants to be a girl's boy toy. Just like you, guys want to be treated as human beings, with dignity and respect.

BACK TO THE GARDEN AGAIN

While at first glance it may appear that this is a new phenomenon, women have long been using sex to gain power and control over men. In fact, this has been going on since biblical times. Remember what happened in the Garden of Eden? The serpent deceived Eve, saying, "You will not surely die.... For God knows that when you eat of it your eyes will be opened, and you will be like God, knowing good and evil" (Genesis 3:4-5). Eve obviously wasn't content to submit to God's way of doing things. She wanted to be like God, possessing more wisdom and power, so she took that catastrophic bite of forbidden fruit. As a consequence for her sin, God told her, "Your desire will be for your husband, *and* he will *rule* over you" (Genesis 3:16, emphasis added).

Since the early days of creation, women have had a love/hate relationship with men, wanting a man's love but resisting the idea that any man should have authority over a woman. In fact, many have fought like crazy for more power for women, sometimes for the right reasons (such as abuse, prejudice, or discrimination) and sometimes for the wrong reasons (such as insecurity, fear, greed, pride, or selfishness). The desire for power—and the belief that power over a man can meet our need for security or love or significance—sometimes drives women to use sex as a bargaining tool in relationships.

Sexual power can be intoxicating, perhaps even addicting, to a young woman. Turning the head of a peer brings a small thrill, while turning the head of an older man holds huge payoffs for the ego, whether it is the captain of the football team, the college professor, or the head of the department at work. This abuse of power can lead to compromising or even forbidden relationships, which we'll talk more about in chapter 18.

WHAT'S BEHIND YOUR PURSUIT OF POWER?

If you are struggling with sexual integrity, you may have an underlying desire for power over men and not even realize it. That was the case for me. But with the help of a trained counselor, I discovered the driving reason behind my inappropriate relationships with men: I was a little girl inside a woman's body, subconsciously seeking a father figure to give me the love I craved.

I spent most of my single days striving to use my appearance as bait to lure guys into feeding my ego. If I was successful in hooking a man with my charms, I secretly felt powerful. But my satisfaction was always short-lived, and before long I was looking for another guy to make me happy.

I always thought my behavior toward men would change after I was married, but it didn't. I started seeing a counselor to understand why I still felt so tempted outside of my marriage. During one of our sessions, my therapist asked me to spend the next week making a list of every man I had ever been with sexually or had pursued emotionally. At the next visit, she asked me to spend a week praying and asking myself, "What do each of these men have in common?" God showed me that each relationship had been with a man who was older than I was and in some form of authority over me—my professor, my boss, my lawyer, and so on.

As I searched my heart to discern why this common thread ran through my relational pursuits, the root of the issue became evident: my hunger for power over a man. Due to my feelings of powerlessness in my relationship with a father who I felt ruled over me with an iron fist, I had subconsciously been recreating authoritative relationships in order to "win this time." Each time I managed to get the upper hand in a relationship, it was really as if I were saying, "See Dad! Someone really does love me! I AM worthy of attention and affection!"

In my attempts to fill the father-shaped hole in my heart and establish some resemblance of self-worth, I was hurting myself. I know from experience that relationships built entirely on sex are devoid of any intimacy or closeness and leave you feeling all the more power *hungry* and power*less*.

I have since discovered the only true source of satisfaction and self-worth—an intimate relationship with my heavenly Father. Since I've been pursuing Him first and foremost, not only has Jesus become my first love and given me a sense of worth beyond what any man could give, He has also restored my relationship with my earthly father and helped me remain faithful to my husband.

Of course the desire for love isn't the only possible motivation behind a desire for power over men. For instance, if you have experienced sexual abuse or emotional neglect from a male, you may desire power over men out of anger, contempt, or a desire to punish anyone who resembles your male abuser. That's what Shelly did—you read her story in chapter 8. Another reason may be fear of being overpowered by a man. Perhaps you assume he's going to try to take advantage of you, so you feel as if you have to overpower him before he overpowers you. Or it may simply be a matter of pride—you may want others to think you are a strong woman and that you have the upper hand in your romantic relationships because you fear being perceived as weak.

"Trying desperately to get a guy's attention might work for a while, but guys who want to stay morally pure will avoid you (which is not your goal) because it eventually becomes obvious that you are too selfish to care about his purity and his relationship with Christ."

—Neil

Do you see a pattern in your own life of aggressively pursuing guys, manipulating and using them for your own pleasure and selfish purposes? If you do, there might be more to it than meets the eye. Ask God to help you discover any underlying motives, and find a wise counselor who can help you gain a healthy understanding of yourself and how to relate with the opposite sex. When you don't have a wise mentor or aren't connected to healthy adults, you can lose your way and find yourself living a life you never intended to live. Don't make that mistake.

RESTORING THE BALANCE OF POWER

To wrap up this chapter, let us provide some balance to this discussion. We're not asking you to become powerless and lay down your rights for any guy so he can walk all over you, sexually or otherwise. Everyone needs a sense of personal power. It's healthy and appropriate to use that power to guard yourself from guys who are seeking to control or coerce you through verbal, physical, or sexual abuse or are insisting that you "put out" for them sexually. Use your power to guard yourself against being taken advantage of and mistreated. But don't use your power to take advantage of others and mistreat them. Do unto others as you would have them do unto you (see Matthew 7:12). Respect others and expect them to respect you.

In closing, we want to let you in on a little secret. Only God can completely satisfy your need for love and power. Does God give His love and power to men?

Yes. But do you need to go through a man to receive it? No. He also gives love and power to women. When you discover how the powerful love of the Holy Spirit can help you live an emotionally healthy, self-controlled, abundantly fulfilled life, you will know that seductive power pales in comparison.

The world doesn't fight fair. But we don't live or fight our battles that way.... The tools of our trade aren't for marketing or manipulation, but they are for demolishing that entire massively corrupt culture. We use our powerful God-tools for smashing warped philosophies, tearing down barriers erected against the truth of God, fitting every loose thought and emotion and impulse into the structure of life shaped by Christ. Our tools are ready at hand for clearing the ground of every obstruction and building lives of obedience into maturity.

2 Corinthians 10:3-6, MSG

dressing to impress

Rather, clothe yourselves with the Lord Jesus Christ, and do not think about how to gratify the desires of the sinful nature.

ROMANS 13:14

You have probably heard gourmet chefs on the cooking channel say that when it comes to food, presentation is everything. Presentation *is* everything, not just with food, but also with your body. We've said it before, and we'll say it again because it is so important: You teach people how to treat you. Either you teach them to treat you with respect or you teach them to treat you with disrespect. Whether you intend to or not, the way you dress—modestly covering the most visually stimulating parts of your body or immodestly revealing as much of your body as you can get away with—sends others a message. If you don't believe us, perhaps your peers will convince you.

After hearing me speak on the radio about the importance of modesty, twenty-year-old Christi, wrote the following in a letter:

When I first began working as a Christian summer camp counselor, I decided that I would refuse to hook up with a guy at camp so I could focus wholeheartedly on the girls in my cabin. I wanted so much for them to like me and to think I was cool that I dressed in the latest young fashions… snug-fitting, low-rise jeans, short shorts, spaghetti-strap tank tops, or tops that were short and clingy enough to resemble the popular crop tops when I was moving around, but long enough that I couldn't be accused of dressing inappropriately. I also taught the girls how to do several of the latest dance moves each night in the cabin, something we all looked forward to and had a lot of fun with.

I succeeded in being well liked by the girls at camp, but I also had the attention and admiration of some of the male camp counselors. I decided that I could just play it cool and clown around with these guys. They chased me around with water guns, gave me piggyback rides to the cafeteria, slipped ice down the back of my shirt, and fun stuff like that. I kept asking them to please leave me alone so I could concentrate on my girls, but they rarely respected my requests, no matter how firm I was.

I complained to one of the other counselors about how the guys were distracting me from what I came to do. She put her hand on mine and sweetly said, "Christi, your actions speak louder than your words. Even though you don't intend to dress to catch guys, they can't avoid noticing you dressing the way you do. If you dress like a cute little plaything and present yourself as a toy, then boys will be boys and try to play with that toy!"

The following year at camp, I took shorts that weren't so short and shirts long enough to be tucked in. Late at night, I taught the girls some worshipful dances to Christian music, and we even performed one in the camp talent show. The boys didn't mess with me much, so I was really able to pour a lot into the girls. I left camp that year feeling so much better about myself than the year before.

Our congratulations to Christi for figuring out that the way she dressed influenced how others viewed her and for changing her wardrobe so that others would treat her with respect.

Rose learned the same lesson when, tired of being invisible to guys, she went to school one day with a bold new look.

You know the saying "Sweet sixteen and never been kissed"? Well, that was me, only I was eighteen and a senior in high school wondering, *What's wrong with me?* I had never been on a date or even asked out. Guys never seemed to notice me, and if they did it was always "only as a friend."

So I saved up my money and purchased a short black skirt, a black spaghetti-strap tank top, a black see-through shirt to go over it, and black knee boots. The next day I fixed my hair all up and put on my makeup a little heavier, with glitter accents. At first I felt a little awkward and wore a T-shirt over it, but it was ruining the effect, so I took it off. People were whispering behind my back and saying that I looked like a hooker. I would probably agree with them, but I had their attention and so I didn't care.

At the end of the day I was walking down a hallway when a guy stopped to talk with me and started rubbing his hands up and down my arms. When I tried to pull away from him and told him to stop, he said, "What's the matter? Isn't this what you want?" That's when I realized how stupid I was being.... No, this was not what I wanted at all. I wanted to be noticed and respected, not noticed and disrespected. Once I got away from him I went to get my T-shirt out of my locker to cover up once again.

Rose and Christi both discovered the hard way that you teach people how to treat you by what you wear. If you want to teach people to treat you with the respect you deserve as a daughter of the King, keep reading.

"Dressing modestly doesn't mean you have to dress like a grandma. Sure, your selection may not be as big, but it's worth the sacrifice. If stores in your area don't carry enough of a variety of modest styles, start a petition and present it to the store manager. When we presented over one thousand names on such a petition to our local mall, store managers formed a committee of teens as fashion consultants and are listening to us since it means more business for them."

—MARIE

FROM SOCIETY INTO THE SANCTUARY

I was walking through a mall one day when I came across a huge display ad, not in Abercrombie & Fitch or Victoria's Secret where I would have expected such an inappropriate graphic display, but in a JCPenney store where I shop with my young children. The ad showed the rear view of a young woman wearing a halter top, low-rise jeans, and thong underwear rising far above the waistline of her pants. I reasoned, *Surely this is just their creative attempt at advertising thongs... Lord knows you can't show a model in one without putting some jeans or something over her behind!*

Thirty minutes later we were in the food court when a young teenager walked by our table strutting her stuff in, you guessed it, low-rise jeans, a high-rise tank top, and thong underwear proudly peeking out from the back. I thought, *So this is the latest trend?* But of course, I never thought it would permeate into the church. However, just a few Sundays later I was dropping off my children at a friend's church, and I couldn't believe what I saw on one of the girls in their youth group—the exact get up!

As a matter of fact, youth pastors tell us, "I'm stunned by how the girls walk into youth group wearing totally immodest clothes! Don't they know they're in church? Don't they know that boys are visually stimulated? Don't they know they give people the wrong impression when they dress seductively for attention?" Unfortunately, too many young women *don't* realize these things, or if they do, they are so desperate for attention (even if it's unhealthy attention) that they ignore wisdom.

But if you want to be a young woman of sexual integrity, you will be different. Smarter. You will teach your guy friends how to treat you with dignity and respect rather than teaching them that you are eye candy or a toy for their sexual jollies. When you catch a young man's eye, it will be because of the way you carry yourself with confidence and character, not because of your skimpy attire. The guy whose head you turn with your inward beauty will more than likely be a godly young man who could possibly make a great husband someday, not some Joe Schmoe who just wants to use your body for his temporary pleasure. You will look to God's Word to determine how you dress, and be an example of purity and modesty for your generation.

SEARCHING THE SCRIPTURES FOR GUIDANCE

While the Bible doesn't have a specific modesty dress code, we can always go back to Jesus' commandment as a guideline for how we treat others, even when it comes to how we are to dress: "Love your neighbor as yourself" (Matthew 22:39).

Picture this scenario: You know your girlfriend is dieting to lose ten pounds before her junior prom. You also know that if she does not lose the weight, her prom dress will be too tight and she will feel uncomfortable all evening. But you have a raging sweet tooth, you are thin and never have to worry about gaining weight, and you love to indulge your cravings in the company of friends. So you insist whenever you go shopping that you and your friend get one of those huge cinnamon rolls at Cinnabon. Plus, you always keep a supply of Krispy Kremes at home, and you bring her one every morning at school. Are you acting lovingly or selfishly toward your friend?

Now consider this: You know that young men are visually stimulated at the sight of a woman's body, especially a scantily clad body (and if you still haven't grasped this truth, we recommend you read *Every Young Man's Battle*!). You may also know that godly young men are trying desperately to bounce their eyes away from sexually stimulating images. Are you acting lovingly or selfishly if you know these things yet insist on wearing clothes that reveal as much of your sleek curves and tanned skin as possible?

> "If you have shirts that are a little too short, try wearing a longer undershirt underneath. It's a very cute style and will keep your midriff covered when you move around."
>
> —BETH

As you are getting dressed each morning, try evaluating what you intend to wear. Ask yourself: Would wearing this outfit be a loving expression, not causing my brothers to stumble and fall?

While Scripture isn't specific about how we are to dress, it does have some specific things to say about the clothing we should wear. Here are a few examples:

Let us behave decently, as in the daytime, not in orgies and drunkenness, not in sexual immorality and debauchery, not in dissension and jealousy. Rather, *clothe yourselves with the Lord Jesus Christ*, and do not think about how to gratify the desires of the sinful nature. (Romans 13:13-14, emphasis added)

Therefore, as God's chosen people, holy and dearly loved, *clothe yourselves with compassion, kindness, humility, gentleness and patience....* And over all these virtues *put on love*, which binds them all together in perfect unity. (Colossians 3:12,14, emphasis added)

All of you, *clothe yourselves with humility* toward one another, because, "God opposes the proud but gives grace to the humble." (1 Peter 5:5, emphasis added)

Notice that the Bible says nothing about bare midriffs and thong underwear! Instead, God tells us to clothe ourselves with Jesus, humility, compassion, kindness, gentleness, patience, and love. Maybe you're thinking, *But I can't wear those to school!* Oh, but you can! Just not by themselves. You must also clothe yourself with actual clothes!

So, how can you translate all this scriptural stuff into practical terms? Read on.

CLEANING OUT YOUR CLOSET

In a day and age when showing more skin is in, when underwear has become outerwear, and Victoria's Secret lingerie is no longer worn secretly, perhaps it's time to rethink your wardrobe. While only you can ultimately decide whether each article of clothing is appropriate or inappropriate, we can offer you help for determining how others are going to be affected by your attire as you walk, bend, reach, and wiggle around throughout the day.

Use the following list of questions to evaluate each article of clothing that you own. A yes answer may mean you need to clean that particular item out of your closet.

Blouses and Tops
- If your blouse buttons up, is it so tight that someone sitting beside you might get a glimpse through the gaps between the buttons as you move around?
- If someone is standing over you or if you are bending over, could that person get an eyeful of cleavage*?
- Are any of your tops so sheer that others can see the lace on your bra?

---

* *cleavage*—the space between a woman's breasts

- Do any of your sleeveless shirts or tank tops reveal your bra straps or require that you not wear a bra?
- Do your shirts reveal any part of your abdomen or back if you do the "hallelujah test" (lift your hands above your head)?
- Do any of your shirts have sexually suggestive slogans (such as "sexy" or "flirt")?

Jeans and Pants

- Are any of your jeans so tight that someone could read the date on the dime in your pocket?
- Do you have to lie down on the bed and suck in your stomach to zip up any of your pants?
- Do any of your jeans ride your hips so low that your underwear can be seen from the back?
- Do you own any pants that have lettering or graphics across the seat to draw attention to your rear view?

> "It's hard to focus on being like Jesus when I see a girl wearing really tight shirts and low-rise jeans. I'm not trying to blame it all on girls because I know we do our fair share of teasing. But I don't want a girlfriend who exposes herself to other guys by dressing immodestly. I want a girl who I can respect and who will respect the fact that I want to guard my eyes against lusting after her body before we are married."
>
> —CURTIS

Skirts and Shorts

- Do your skirts or shorts come above your thumbnail when your arms are at your side?
- Back up to a full-length mirror and then bend over to touch your toes. Are your private parts or panties on display in this position?
- Do any of your skirts ride excessively high above the knee when you are seated?

- When you are wearing a particular skirt, could someone sitting or standing in front of you catch a glimpse of your panties or upper thighs if you fail to keep your legs crossed?
- Regardless of the length of your skirts, do any have slits up the front, back, or side that could draw a guy's eye too far up your legs?

Undergarments

- If you choose to wear thong underwear, does the waistband show when you squat down or bend over?
- Do you have bras that you like to wear because you know the pretty straps will show when you wear certain tops?

If all of your clothes pass this test, you can be confident that you are dressing modestly. Clothed in righteousness, modesty, and dignity, you'll be dressing to impress young men who are truly worth impressing!

 She is clothed with strength and dignity; she can laugh at the days to come.

Proverbs 31:25

to flirt or not to flirt

Words from a wise [woman's] mouth are gracious, but a fool is consumed by [her] own lips. At the beginning [her] words are folly; at the end they are wicked madness.

ECCLESIASTES 10:12-13

Many young women think that because they are "only flirting," they're not hurting anyone. But is this true? Is flirting always an innocent, fun game?

Alicia, Rachel, and Diana used to think so, but they don't anymore. Experience has taught them that flirting can lead to compromising and even dangerous situations. See if you agree after hearing where flirting led them.

LOOK...BUT DON'T TOUCH!

Alicia and a guy friend were flirting with each other after youth group one evening when no one else was around. Although she was acting seductively "just for fun," he had more on his mind than just flirting, and began to get aggressive with her. He forced her up against a wall, pressed his body into hers and began to kiss her. Shocked and disgusted, she managed to get away. She sums up the lesson she learned with these words:

> My just wanting to flirt for attention and have fun at the expense of a guy's hormonal surge turned out to be a dangerous, not-so-fun experience.

Rachel had a similar experience when she was working as a hostess at a nice restaurant the summer she graduated from high school. The bartender was an "absolutely gorgeous Mel Gibson look-alike," and she loved how attractive and sexy she felt when he flirted with her. Rachel started dressing provocatively to gain even more attention from him and felt rewarded when he told her how "hot" she was looking. She considered it all fun and games until one day after work when he asked her to walk him to his truck. She tells this story:

> We talked a few minutes and then he asked if I wanted to go for a ride with
> him. I knew I probably shouldn't go, but I didn't want to lose his attention,
> so I went. He drove down an alley behind a gas station and began to kiss me.
> I told him to stop, but he said there was no way I could expect him to take
> no for an answer after everything I had been saying to him to drive him
> crazy. Even though all my clothes stayed on, it was still a very traumatic
> experience, and I ended up quitting my job to get away from him and that
> bitter memory.

When Diana was fourteen she and her friends made a game of trying to attract the attention of older guys. One year at winter camp, she met an eighteen-year-old from one of the other churches at the camp, and he immediately started paying her lots of attention, which she loved. She knew her parents wouldn't approve of her seeing a guy that old, but she figured they'd never know what she did at camp, and what they didn't know wouldn't hurt them. Diana says:

> After a while I started noticing little things that should have been a warning
> for me to back off, but I didn't. For instance, he would touch me a lot; he
> hugged me tightly for a long time whenever we saw each other; he would
> sit very close to me in the sessions. Sometimes he would want me to sit on
> his lap, facing him. As camp went on, I began to feel uncomfortable about
> the things he did that had excited me. He started saying sexual things to
> me, and on the last day, he gave me one of his tight hugs and then slowly
> moved his hands down my back and grabbed my behind. I wanted to be
> offended, but I knew I had led him on with my flirting.

Alicia, Rachel, and Diana realized that it's no innocent game to behave seductively and play with a guy's mind in the name of fun.

Even though Alicia, Rachel, and Diana were just "having fun," their flirting led these guys to believe they were interested in a romantic or physical relationship with them—and the guys acted on that belief. (Duh!) Even though they had intentionally tried to make these guys' eyes pop out of their heads with seductive remarks and behaviors, they also intended for the guys to look but not touch. Do you see why certain kinds of flirting are cruel to a guy—and cruel for him to do to you?

But What If I Do Like Him?

At this point you may be wondering, *But what if I am attracted to a guy? Can't I act friendly toward him and let him know I like him?* Yes you can, as long as

- your behavior and/or words aren't sexually suggestive, seductive, or clearly unwanted;
- his age is an appropriate match for your age;
- he is available (not married or seeing anyone);
- he has no significant character concerns (and is a Christian with like-minded values); and
- those who know you best and love you most—your parents and friends—support the relationship.

If you want to be a young woman of sexual and emotional integrity, your actions will line up with your heart, and you won't mislead a guy by sending him messages that you're interested in him when you aren't. You'll also want to consider what Scripture says about such behavior.

Searching the Scriptures

While you won't find the word *flirting* in the Bible, that doesn't mean God is silent in this matter. He cares very much about the messages we communicate with our words and our actions. Consider these verses and how they apply to flirting:

> For out of the overflow of the heart the mouth speaks. The good [woman]
> brings good things out of the good stored up in [her], and the evil [woman]

brings evil things out of the evil stored up in [her]. But I tell you that [women] will have to give account on the day of judgment for every careless word they have spoken. For by your words you will be [found innocent], and by your words you will be [found guilty]. (Matthew 12:34-37)

What do your words spoken to the opposite sex reveal about your character and heart?

But among you there must not be even a hint of sexual immorality, or of any kind of impurity, or of greed, because these are improper for God's holy people. Nor should there be obscenity, foolish talk or coarse joking, which are out of place, but rather thanksgiving. (Ephesians 5:3-4)

Can you honestly say that your words and actions do not reflect even a hint of sexual immorality?

When we put bits into the mouths of horses to make them obey us, we can turn the whole animal. Or take ships as an example. Although they are so large and are driven by strong winds, they are steered by a very small rudder wherever the pilot wants to go. Likewise the tongue is a small part of the body, but it makes great boasts. Consider what a great forest is set on fire by a small spark. The tongue also is a fire, a world of evil among the parts of the body. It corrupts the whole person, sets the whole course of his life on fire. (James 3:3-6)

Did you catch that last part? The tongue "corrupts the whole person." If you want to be a young woman of sexual and emotional integrity, match your words, thoughts, actions, and convictions with God's Word. Remember what we talked about in chapter 3? When all four of these things agree with one another and align with the Word of God, we are acting with sexual and emotional integrity. But if any one area is out of alignment with God's Word, we have compromised our sexual integrity, regardless of how far we've gone physically.

Here's one of our favorite verses, which promises that when we choose our words carefully to reflect the pure love of our Savior, we will be rewarded with His favor and friendship:

> [She] who loves a pure heart and whose speech is gracious
>   will have the king for [her] friend. (Proverbs 22:11)

Your words matter to God—both what you say and how you say it.

A FILTER FOR OUR WORDS AND ACTIONS

Now that you have a better understanding of what inappropriate flirting is, how it can be cruel and dangerous, and how God feels about how you use your words, let's examine how you can ensure that your words and actions seek the best interests of others and how you can avoid "any hint of sexual immorality."

If you aren't sure whether your behavior with a guy is inappropriately flirtatious, ask yourself the following questions. They can help you determine whether your words and actions are in a guy's best interest or if they are in the interest of your own ego.

- What do I hope to gain by saying or doing this? Will these words or actions ultimately be harmful to either of us or beneficial to both of us?
- Is this guy seeing someone? If so, would his girlfriend get upset with me if she knew I was speaking to her boyfriend in this way?
- Are these words going to tempt him into coming around me more often than he should? Am I arousing him sexually?
- Am I using words or actions to manipulate this person into meeting my emotional needs and making me feel better about myself?
- If I actually say what I am thinking about saying or do what I am thinking about doing, then turn around to find one of my parents, siblings, or friends standing there, would I have some explaining to do?
- If I sense that a guy I'm not really interested in is flirting with me, am I making it more fun for him by playing his game, or am I maintaining my own personal convictions about guarding my mouth and his heart?

We also recommend that you:

- Ignore any guy who starts making eyes at you, shouting (like "Hey, baby!"), or tries to get your attention in inappropriate ways. Pretend you don't even hear him and refuse to look his direction. All he wants is your attention, and if you give it to him, even if you're just telling him off for treating you with such disrespect, you are playing right into his hands. Actions speak louder than words. If he gets absolutely no response from you, he'll get your drift that you are not a girl to be toyed with, and he'll think twice about embarrassing himself like that again around you.

- When talking with a guy on the phone, do not say anything sexually suggestive. A good rule of thumb is to keep from saying anything you would be embarrassed for someone else to overhear. Also, avoid talking on the phone with a guy after bedtime hours. These late-night private conversations usually open the door for fueling sexual passions.

- Direct any conversation or questions regarding sexual issues to a parent or trusted mentor, such as a counselor, youth pastor, or same-gender teacher. Avoid discussing sexual matters with peers, especially the opposite sex. They usually don't know any more than you do about sexual issues and can quickly mislead you into lowering your sexual standards to their level, which may be very low. Such conversations can also be misinterpreted as flirting, can be very arousing to you or to others, and can open the door for physical temptations. The only exception to this rule is a female accountability partner whom you know will sharpen you and challenge you to consistently do the right thing.

RUNNING TO THE SAFEST PLACE

The next time you are tempted to flirt "just for fun," remember that there is Someone you can whisper your heart's desires to and have fun with who isn't going to jeopardize your integrity but instead strengthen it. If you are looking for a safe relationship to pour your attentions and affections into, you don't have to look any further than Jesus Christ. He can delight your heart and soul and satisfy every fiber of your being much more than any boy on the planet.

If you are thinking, *No way will talking to God ever excite me like talking to a guy,* then you haven't allowed yourself to be courted by our Creator. The same God whose words possessed the power to form the entire universe longs to whisper words into your heart that have the power to thrill you, heal you, and draw you into a deeper love relationship than you ever imagined possible. A guy may say that you look good, but God says He is "enthralled by your beauty" (Psalm 45:11). A boyfriend may tell you, "Of course I love you," but God says, "I have loved you with an everlasting love; I have drawn you with loving-kindness" (Jeremiah 31:3). Even your future husband may tell you, "I'm committed to you until death," but God says to you right now, "Never will I leave you; never will I forsake you" (Hebrews 13:5) and that not even death can separate you from His love that is in Christ Jesus (see Romans 8:38-39).

Make time to connect with God and say all the things that you'd say to a boyfriend or a best friend. Speak whatever is on your heart, and then listen as God speaks straight from His heart to yours. Make time to get to know Him intimately. Not only will He reveal Himself to you, He'll also help you get to know yourself better and show you the secrets to satisfying your innermost desires for genuine love and intimacy. He knows your needs better than you know them yourself, and He wants to satisfy you fully and completely.

 May the words of my mouth and the meditation of my heart be pleasing in your sight, O LORD, my Rock and my Redeemer.

Psalm 19:14

PART IV

guarding your mind

winning the mental battle

> When I want to do good, evil is right there with me. For in my inner
> being I delight in God's law; but I see another law at work in the mem-
> bers of my body, waging war against the law of my mind and making
> me a prisoner of the law of sin.
>
> ROMANS 7:21-23

In the movie *What Women Want,* Nick Marshall, played by Mel Gibson, develops a telepathic ability to hear each thought, opinion, and desire that goes through every woman's head. While the plot is far-fetched, it gives food for thought.

How would you feel if every guy you encountered had the ability to read your mind, just by being in your presence? Does that possibility make you nervous? You bet it does! Especially when you consider the thoughts that you would never tell anyone about such as these:

- *I wonder if he thinks I'm pretty?*
- *Whoa! He's hot!*
- *What would it be like to kiss him?*
- *Could he be The One?*

And what if every female developed this ability too? She may hear these private thoughts of yours:

- *She really thinks she's something, doesn't she?*
- *How did she get a cute guy like that?*
- *I wonder if her boyfriend would be interested in me if they ever break up?*
- *At least I'm not that fat!*

Even though you can rest assured that others aren't likely to develop this ability anytime soon, you have an even bigger concern. God has had it all along.

What's on the inside of your heart and mind? Could you, like David, be so bold as to pray such a thing as this: "Test me, O LORD, and try me, examine my heart and my mind" (Psalm 26:2)? Notice David didn't say, "Examine my actions." He asked God to examine what he was *thinking*.

Even young women who have never had a serious relationship or been involved in sexual activity often have impure thoughts and longings. Regardless of our past, all of us share in this struggle.

No matter how well any of us try to prevent tempting thoughts from entering the gate of our mind, some will still slip through. Life itself brings temptation. The day you stop experiencing temptation isn't the day you stop reading romance novels or watching MTV and R-rated movies. It isn't the day you put a wedding band on your finger—or even the day you fast and pray for twelve hours straight. The day you stop experiencing temptation is the day you die. Temptation comes part and parcel with being human, and you are no exception to that rule.

But just because everyone has tempting thoughts doesn't mean that it is wise to indulge in them or entertain them. You can't stop a thought from popping into your mind, and God understands this. However, you can refuse to entertain such thoughts. As this famous quote says:

> Sow a thought, reap an action;
> Sow an action, reap a habit;
> Sow a habit, reap a character;
> Sow a character, reap a destiny.
> —Samuel Smiles

If you want to be a young woman of sexual and emotional integrity, you'll want your thoughts to reap positive actions and habits so you might better reflect a Christlike character and fulfill God's destiny for your life. To help you understand how to do this, let's examine three questions about your thought life:

1. What effect do your thoughts have on your battle for sexual and emotional integrity?
2. How can you guard your mind against influences that cause you to sin?
3. What does the Bible say you should focus your mind on, and how is that possible?

THINKING EQUALS REHEARSING

To help answer the question about what effect your thoughts have on you, imagine an actor preparing to perform in a play. She memorizes her lines, gets inside the character's head, and tries to understand how this person would feel and act. She rehearses being that person. She thinks intently about doing what that person would do and saying what that person would say, exactly the way she would say it. The more she's rehearsed being that character, the sharper and more "automatic" her performance.

Something similar happens when you fantasize about sexually or emotionally inappropriate behavior. You are rehearsing when you imagine the conversations you would have with someone if you were ever alone with that individual. You are rehearsing when you envision a sexually intimate encounter. You are rehearsing when you envision what you'll say and do in these encounters. Rehearsing makes you susceptible to acting out the scenarios you have been fantasizing about. It feeds your desire and breaks down your resistance. So when Satan lays the trap and presents you with a similar compromising situation, guess what? More than likely you will play the part exactly the way you have rehearsed it. If you don't guard your mind, you'll find that when it comes to your relationships with the opposite sex, your resistance can be low before any encounter takes place.

But you do have some choice in this matter—you don't have to be a sitting duck for Satan's darts. You can train your mind to mind.

TRAINING YOUR MIND TO MIND

One of my favorite sayings is: You *can't* keep a bird from flying over your head, but you *can* keep it from building a nest in your hair! The same can be said about temptation.

For instance, perhaps one of your friends has a really cute boyfriend and you feel tempted to stay after class to chat with him, just to see where the conversation may lead. (Secretly you wonder if he could grow to like you more than her.) Or maybe your favorite teacher stirs your spirit, and you think for a moment about how intriguing it would be to pick his brilliant brain over lunch, even though he could be fired for socializing with a student. Maybe a guy's football uniform makes you wonder for a fleeting moment what he looks like without it on. Again, such random thoughts are not sin, but dwelling on inappropriate or sexual fantasies *is* sin and increases the likelihood that you will act on such thoughts in the future. You can't keep from being tempted, but you can avoid rehearsing, and you can certainly refuse to act out a tempting thought. You can train your mind to mind. No temptation becomes sin without your permission.

So how do you keep the bird from building a nest in your hair? What do you do when you come face to face with tempting thoughts? And how do you avoid rehearsing them?

Bouncing Your Thoughts

As mentioned in chapter 4, Scripture tells us that Jesus was tempted, even sexually, but that He was also sinless.

> For we do not have a high priest who is unable to sympathize with our
> weaknesses, but we have one who has been tempted in every way, just as we
> are—yet was without sin. Let us then approach the throne of grace with con-
> fidence, so that we may receive mercy and find grace to help us in our time
> of need. (Hebrews 4:15-16)

Jesus understands what it feels like to be tempted. He was human too. He underwent the same kinds of temptations you experience in relationships, yet He did not give in to any of them. If you have the Holy Spirit living in you, you can have the same victory as you learn to resist temptation.

You can bounce inappropriate thoughts right out of your brain by rehearsing appropriate responses to them. For instance, if you suddenly imagine yourself getting sexual with your date, bounce that thought by imagining how you will respond if he starts French kissing you or asks you to do something sexual. Practice in your mind how you will politely refuse to go there. Instead of envisioning how you can manipulate your boyfriend into being alone with you, imagine how much fun you can have together in a public setting. In your mind's eye, see yourself nipping any unhealthy obsession in the bud. Bounce unhealthy thoughts out of your mind and usher in healthy ones.

You can also rebuke temptation by mentally rehearsing how to communicate to a guy that you are not to be toyed with or that you are not emotionally needy:

- *Imagine how you would respond if your best friend's boyfriend approached you while you are alone and said that he's always thought you were pretty.* Rather than flirting back or entertaining thoughts that would betray your friend, imagine simply telling him, "Thank you," and walking to where others are gathered.

- *Say that a handsome guy at work says you are so hot that thoughts of you make him have to take a cold shower.* Rather than being flattered by such an inappropriate sexual remark, simply envision yourself giving him an appropriate reply such as, "I don't appreciate that kind of comment," and walking away. If something like this actually occurs and your reply doesn't deter him, inform your boss that you are being sexually harassed.

- *Suppose a cute guy asks you out, but he has a bad reputation and doesn't believe in God.* Rather than considering all the ways you could "change him with your love" and imagining what it would be like to date him, envision yourself replying, "I appreciate your asking, but no thank you."

- *Imagine that a much older guy begins flirting with you and inviting you to meet up with him after school.* Rather than thinking about how much you'd like to go out with him, imagine politely telling him something like, "I'm sorry, but I'm not interested."

Another way to battle inappropriate thoughts is to redirect them.

REDIRECTING TEMPTING THOUGHTS

Here are some specific examples to get you thinking in the right direction.

- When you see a good-looking guy, resist the urge to fantasize about him. Simply say to yourself, *Lord, You sure know how to create awesome works!* and then move on with your focus on God instead of some guy.

- When an inappropriate or sinful thought comes into your mind, redirect it by meditating on verses you have memorized as a way to keep your focus where it needs to be. The following verses are good ones:

To [her] who overcomes, I will give the right to sit with me on my throne, just as I overcame and sat down with my Father on his throne. (Revelation 3:21)

Even a fool is thought wise if [she] keeps silent, and discerning if [she] holds [her] tongue. (Proverbs 17:28)

Do not conform any longer to the pattern of this world, but be transformed by the renewing of your mind. Then you will be able to test and approve what God's will is—his good, pleasing and perfect will. (Romans 12:2)

- Sing a song in your mind that helps you resist temptation. ZOEgirl's "Dismissed" and Rebecca St. James's "Wait for Me" are two examples of songs that can help keep your thoughts where they need to be.
- Instead of entertaining sexual or inappropriate thoughts about a guy, pray for his future wife. Or pray for the husband you may have someday. Remind yourself that entertaining inappropriate or sexual thoughts about this person may create emotional baggage you wouldn't be proud to bring into your future marriage relationship. Thank God that with His help you are able to keep your heart and mind pure.
- Finally, as my coauthor, Steve, says on his radio program *New Life Live*, when you come face to face with temptation, simply do the next *right* thing. Were you on your way to the bus stop when you encountered this hottie? Then do not hesitate. Catch that bus. Were you heading to meet a girlfriend to study? Don't keep her waiting. Go. If you want to remain on the path toward righteousness, don't allow yourself to get sidetracked by a handsome guy if this is a relationship you should not entertain.

What is your game plan for rebuking and redirecting tempting thoughts? How will you respond when that bird flies overhead? Will you shoo it away, or will you allow it to build a nest in your hair? One of the main ways you can shoo it away is by maintaining your focus on the Creator (God) rather than focusing on the creation (cute guys!).

KEEPING THE MAIN THING THE MAIN THING

We've mentioned it before, but do you recall what Jesus said is by far the most important thing in life?

> "Love the Lord your God with all your heart and with all your soul and
> with all your mind." This is the first and greatest commandment.
> (Matthew 22:37-38)

This verse doesn't say Jesus wants you to love the Lord with *whatever is left* of your heart, soul, and mind. Nor does it say you should sit around all day and meditate on God. He knows you have a life. He's the One who gave it to you, and He wants you to be the best student, daughter, sister, and friend possible.

According to these verses, Jesus wants us to love God *more* than any of the other things that demand our time and attention. We are to love God above anything else in this world, with as much strength and passion as each of us possibly can. We demonstrate this love for God by focusing our thoughts and energies on those things He's prepared for us to do and that are pleasing to Him. God wants us to do what Paul encouraged the people of Philippi to do:

> Whatever is true, whatever is noble, whatever is right, whatever is pure,
> whatever is lovely, whatever is admirable—if anything is excellent or praise-
> worthy—think about such things. (Philippians 4:8)

Here's how a young woman who loves God and lives to serve Him might put this verse into practice: She rolls out of bed to prepare for her day, trying to look her best to give a positive impression to the people she encounters, because she knows she represents God. She might spend a few minutes reading her Bible, praying, or singing songs to the Lord as she curls her hair in front of the bathroom mirror. As she eats breakfast, puts the finishing touches on her homework, and packs her backpack for school, she is preparing to be a responsible student. As she focuses on her teachers and tries to learn as much as possible, she does so in order to maximize the potential God has placed inside her.

As she goes from class to class, she's got her radar up to see if there's a girlfriend who needs some encouragement. If she has a friend who doesn't know Jesus at all, she looks for opportunities to show that person what He looks like through her attitudes and actions. As she writes a note of congratulations to a classmate who just made the cheerleading squad, forwards a funny e-mail to her friend, or calls to check in on her grandmother, she does it all to build and maintain healthy and positive relationships.

Are we saying that God is supposed to be the only thing you think about? No. But we are saying that as you think on the things that daily demand your attention, you can still love God with all your heart, soul, and mind and share His love with others. When you demonstrate responsible stewardship of the life He has given you, your life offers undeniable proof of your love for Him.

He will keep in perfect peace all those who trust in him, whose thoughts turn often to the Lord!

Isaiah 26:3, TLB

a healthy starvation diet

> Put to death, therefore, whatever belongs to your earthly nature: sexual immorality, impurity, lust, evil desires and greed, which is idolatry. Because of these, the wrath of God is coming.
>
> COLOSSIANS 3:5-6

Inside every Christian two opposing forces fight each other. The Bible refers to these two forces as our flesh and our spirit. While Christians take delight in God's law, we also continue to battle the "law of sin," which causes us to crave ungodly things. Paul wrote of these two laws at work within us in his letter to the Romans:

> So I find this law at work: When I want to do good, evil is right there with me. For in my inner being I delight in God's law; but I see another law at work in the members of my body, waging war against the law of my mind and making me a prisoner of the law of sin at work within my members. What a wretched man I am! Who will rescue me from this body of death? Thanks be to God—through Jesus Christ our Lord! (7:21-25)

Sound familiar? Have you ever tried to stop doing something that you knew was wrong but just couldn't stop? Ever tried to be more disciplined in a certain area of your life, only to cave under pressure?

These battles are fairly predictable. When both good and evil battle within you, do you know who will eventually take the prize? When your flesh wrestles with your spirit, do you know who will eventually win? *Whichever one you feed the most.*

If you feast on MTV and romance novels, you can bet that your flesh takes control when you face sexual temptations. However, if you feast on God's Word, prayer, and healthy relationships with godly people, your spirit can consistently overpower your flesh, even in the midst of fierce temptations.

Who do you want to feed the most—your flesh or your spirit?

GARBAGE IN, GARBAGE OUT

While you might think that you can watch trashy television shows, listen to raunchy music, or even look at pornography without any negative effects, I am living proof that when garbage is put into your brain, it rots and causes a stench in your life. When I was twelve I started soaking up the soap operas each summer. From 11:30 a.m. to 3:00 p.m., five days a week, I faithfully watched *Ryan's Hope, All My Children, One Life to Live,* and *General Hospital.*

As I reflect on that season of my life, I can see a direct parallel between what I was allowing into my mind and what was coming out of my life. *Ryan's Hope* didn't exactly give me any hope of living a pure lifestyle. I'm surprised I didn't have any children before I got married, as much as I watched *All My Children.* I'm also thankful that I didn't lose my "one life to live" because of sexually transmitted diseases, and I should have been admitted to a "general hospital," as lovesick as I often was.

My idol in those years was Erica Cane, Susan Lucci's character on *All My Children.* Her seductive style fascinated me as men fell at her feet. Even as early as the sixth grade, I began practicing her tricks of the trade by convincing boys that lying to our parents and meeting at the movies wasn't really a date.

I spent my summers watching the soaps, but twenty years ago it took a rocket scientist to program a VCR, so I was in soap-opera withdrawal while school was in session. However, I quickly found a substititue when a friend introduced me to teen romance novels. I would sit in class with my romance training manual nestled between the pages of my history textbook pages, mentally rehearsing how to manipulate and seduce young men into giving me love and attention. By the time I graduated from college ten years later, my list of sexual relationships would have made even a soap-opera character's mouth drop open. Even though I was a Christian, I fed my flesh much more than I fed my Spirit, and as a result, my flesh controlled my sexual choices.

A DANGEROUS DIET

I learned the hard way that when you fill your mind with sexual images, you awaken sexual desires that should only be entertained and fulfilled within marriage. So did Chrissie. She began reading her mom's romance novels and soon found that they not only stimulated her emotionally but also stimulated her sexually. Chrissie explains:

> Sometimes I hold a romance novel in one hand while masturbating with the other. I am too scared and ashamed to ask anyone about what I am thinking and feeling. No one talks about this stuff at church, so I often wonder, *Am I the only one who thinks like this?*

Even though Chrissie feels alone in her struggle, she's certainly not. No temptation seizes you that isn't common to other women (see 1 Corinthians 10:13), and fantasy and masturbation are certainly two of the most common.

Sadly, some young women allow their mental fantasies to become their reality. Such was the case with Whitney's sister. The two of them used to love watching MTV and teen soaps—*Melrose Place, Dawson's Creek,* and old episodes of *Beverly Hills 90210,* but Whitney stopped when she heard a youth pastor talk about the problems that can result from putting such images into our minds. Unfortunately, her sister didn't. Whitney told us her sad story:

> When my sister was sixteen, she was dressing like Madonna and other pop stars and had a steady boyfriend who hung out at the house a lot. By the time she turned seventeen, she found out she was pregnant. She had to drop out of school because she felt so sick. Her boyfriend refused to have anything to do with her or the baby, and she had to give the baby up for adoption. She lost most of her friends and no guys ever ask her out. Unfortunately, she still watches some of the stuff that I think got her into all this trouble in the first place.

Whitney sounds like a wise young woman. It's tragic when someone we love has her entire world turned upside down as a result of negative media influences, yet still refuses to give them up.

While we don't know of anyone who intentionally becomes addicted to pornography, we have met young people who innocently stumbled onto a pornographic movie or Web site, and rather than immediately turning it off and bouncing their thoughts, they watched it, only to find how addicting it can be. Jen says that this is what happened to her.

Late one night she was channel surfing in her room and came across a show that looked like *Baywatch*. A guy and girl were on a beach, and he was giving her mouth to mouth, like he had just saved her from drowning. Jen was shocked when they started doing sexual things that you don't normally see on a television show. Even when she realized it was a pornographic movie, she kept watching the film, and then another and another that night. She began staying up after everyone had gone to bed, just to watch that channel. Jen shares this:

> Several weeks later, I freaked out when my mom woke me up at 2 a.m., asking, "What are you watching, young lady?" I had been watching porn movies, but I was too afraid to admit what I had been doing, so I lied. I said that I had been watching a prime-time type television show earlier and had fallen asleep around 10 p.m. before the channel turned to porn. My mom believed me, but I've always felt bad about it. It did put the fear of God in me that I should never look at that kind of stuff again, and I haven't. I just wish I could get the images out of my mind.

We wish we knew of a quick fix that would help Jen rid her mind of such images, but we don't. That's one of the frightening things about pornography—even when you aren't viewing it, the images flash on the screen of your mind.

It's also disturbing how pornography can suddenly land right in front of your eyes, even when you are not looking for it. Kaylie had no idea that she was about to view a pornographic message when she opened an e-mail with the subject line: "Girls Who Just Want to Have Fun!" She thought it was a cartoon or a message from a friend. When she saw it was pornography, she thought it was funny and showed it to a classmate in computer lab. Her classmate then told her about some porn Web sites where she could see similar images. Before she knew it, Kaylie says she was hooked:

> At first, I went to some of those sites just for the shock value and to laugh at them, but then I found myself drawn to looking at that kind of stuff all the time. At night I think about those pictures, and I sometimes even get up in the middle of the night to surf the Internet for other sites. I'm worried that maybe I'm addicted to them, because I can't seem to stop.

Jen and Kaylie discovered what too many young women are discovering the hard way—pornography can be addicting and consume your mind with thoughts that continue to plague you, even when your eyes are closed.

GO ON A STARVATION DIET

If you have a steady diet of messages in the media that weaken your defenses in the battle for sexual integrity, we strongly urge you to go on a starvation diet. When you starve your appetite for sin, it loses its power over you. Then your hunger for righteousness and purity begin driving your thoughts, actions, and attitudes.

To starve yourself, simply do these things:

- *Decide not to watch daytime or evening soap operas.* Soaps that are popular with teens such as *Melrose Place, Charmed, Dawson's Creek,* and *The O.C.* usually portray sex outside of marriage as something *everyone* is doing and as socially acceptable. But the characters on such shows rarely deal with unplanned pregnancy, sexually transmitted diseases, low self-esteem, depression, spiritual conviction, and all the other things that come along with premarital sex. Of course, soap operas are not the only television shows that portray sex outside of marriage as acceptable, and we'll discuss those in the following chapter as well as some ways to discern between appropriate and inappropriate television programs.
- *Avoid watching television talk shows that make a mockery out of God's plan for sex.* Although it can be entertaining to hear all the shocking details of

other people's sex lives on such programs as *Jerry Springer, Maury,* and *Jenny Jones,* we believe these shows are a huge waste of time and do much more harm than good. The topics of these shows are too often something along the lines of "Whose fake boobs look better?" "Who's had sex with whom?" "Who's my baby's daddy?" If our only choices were watching these shows or complete boredom, we'd choose boredom every time. Surely you can find better things to do with your time than watching shows like these.

- *Choose not to read steamy romance novels.* We consider these to be pornography for females. The sexually graphic scenarios are taken in mentally and stir us emotionally, which can be even more alluring to women than visual images. They usually glamorize sex outside of marriage and can easily arouse you sexually. They also can set you up for disappointment in future romantic relationships and even later in marriage, because romance novels do not reflect real-life relationships. If your idea of the perfect mate or the perfect relationship is formed by reading romance novels, you are setting yourself up for disillusionment down the road.

- *Don't watch MTV.* Consider that 75 percent of videos shown on MTV that tell a story involve sexual imagery, over 50 percent involve violence, and 80 percent combine the two, suggesting violence against women.[1] We believe that is reason enough to avoid MTV altogether, as we certainly don't want to feed that kind of garbage into our brains and allow it to infect our lives. A great alternative would be to find some good Christian music video stations. Gone are the days when Christian music paled in comparison to the edgy sounds of contemporary music. These days Christian music easily competes with any rock, pop, country, heavy metal, or alternative group out there. These video channels can be just as entertaining as anything else on the market, and oftentimes more so.

- *Avoid looking at any form of pornography, whether it is in print, on film, or on the Internet.* Pornography is anything visual or auditory that is intended to be sexually provocative or depicts sexual activity in a graphic way. Magazines, movies, Web sites, and even telephone hotlines can be pornographic.

Psalm 101:3 says, "I will set before my eyes no vile thing." Viewing these images merely creates a battle in your brain, one that you'll have to fight all your life. After you marry, you'll more than likely have to disconnect from the mental pictures you've stored in your memory to connect fully with your husband. You don't want to have your sexual desires awakened prior to marriage, right? You don't want your future sexual focus distracted away from your husband by the memory of couples in pornographic scenes, right? Then rather than allowing pornography to control you, control your desire to feed your flesh with such images.

Share the Secret

When you refuse to look at, read, or listen to these forms of sex-saturated media, you strengthen your ability to resist temptation. Allow only healthy messages to come into your mind—messages that are going to equip you to lead the kind of truly fulfilling, God-honoring life that you desire to live.

Sadly, many of your peers don't know this secret to living a truly fulfilling, healthy life. Dr. Ann Kearney-Cooke says:

> The culture—MTV videos and television shows—helps to reduce adolescent girls to being successful when they look sexy and date often.... There is a status to the girl in middle school who is the first one to start dating. Teenagers feast on media images while they starve for love and parental attention. One of the ways we learn about relationships is by being in them and seeing them at work. Today, kids come home from school and the parents or parent might not be home. They watch MTV and talk shows and cruise the Internet, and that is where they are learning about relationships.[2]

We want to challenge you to share the secret with your friends of guarding your mind and winning the mental battle. Encourage your friends to look to the real world and to God's Word for how to have great relationships rather than looking to the media. Invite them to your church, where they can get to know people who are happily married and living the fulfilling life that we all want to live.

Be the kind of young woman who sets great examples in your own friendships and dating relationships. Then you'll accomplish three great goals: guarding yourself, guiding others, and glorifying God.

You were taught, with regard to your former way of life, to put off your old self, which is being corrupted by its deceitful desires; to be made new in the attitude of your minds; and to put on the new self, created to be like God in true righteousness and holiness.

Ephesians 4:22-24

mastering the media

Therefore, I urge you, [sisters], in view of God's mercy, to offer your bodies as living sacrifices, holy and pleasing to God—this is your spiritual act of worship. Do not conform any longer to the pattern of this world, but be transformed by the renewing of your mind. Then you will be able to test and approve what God's will is—his good, pleasing and perfect will.

Romans 12:1-2

Have you ever heard of the science experiment with a frog and hot water? The experiment goes like this: You put a frog into a pot of boiling water, and he immediately jumps out, recognizing that it isn't a safe place to be. Then, you place the same frog into a pot of room-temperature water and slowly bring the pot to a boil. What happens? The frog becomes a dinner entrée of boiled frog legs because his body gradually adjusts to the temperature of his environment. The frog is *gradually desensitized to* (unable to feel) the danger.

We, too, can become gradually desensitized to danger, not to the danger of boiling water but to the danger of our purity being compromised through the media. As a society, we have become so desensitized to sexual messages that we often unscrew our heads, put them under the La-Z-Boy recliner, and allow the television and other forms of media to fill our minds with worldly scripts.

I once recorded two hours of prime-time television shows, and then edited the tape down to a twelve-minute clip of nothing but the sexual innuendoes* surrounded by enough of the story line to make them entertaining to watch. When I

---

* *innuendoes*—comments with hidden sexual hints or suggestions

show the video clip to teens, I challenge them to count all the sexual messages they see or hear during that twelve-minute clip.

Guess what happens every time? The audience catches the first three or four innuendoes, but then becomes so engrossed in the funny scenes that they stop counting. Most people in the audience count ten or eleven sexual innuendoes. The actual number? Forty-one. Even the adults in the room do not usually recognize more than 50 percent of these sexual messages.

In the previous chapter we discussed some forms of media that should be resisted altogether—soap operas, trashy talk shows, romance novels, MTV, and all forms of pornography—but what about the other kinds of media? We get bombarded every day with messages, sometimes good ones, other times, not so good. In this chapter we encourage you to evaluate the subtle messages being promoted in the media—whether through television, music, movies, magazines, or something on the Internet—so you can be wise about what you allow to enter your mind.

First, let's take a look at some of the messages promoted through television, magazines, and the music industry.

MESSAGES FROM TELEVISION

We recently surfed through the channels to see what's on these days. Here's what we found.

- On an episode of *Friends,* Rachel (Jennifer Aniston) reminds guest star Winona Ryder of how they used to make out with each other when they were younger by kissing her passionately once again. Curious as to what the big deal is, Phoebe (Lisa Kudrow) spontaneously steals a kiss from Rachel, but then declares, "Ahh, I've had better!"
- On one of the first episodes of the sitcom *I'm with Her,* Patrick, a teacher, begins dating glamorous movie star Alex Young. The theme of the show is that Alex is jealous of Patrick's previous live-in lover, but the running joke throughout the show is how everyone (including Patrick and Alex) expect their third date to be "the special night" where he lights the "sex candle" and they stop "just talking."

- On *It's All Relative,* an engaged couple argues over the fact that she doesn't like his boots and he doesn't like her nightgown. "I thought you like my snuggle-bunny nightie!" she says, to which he responds, "I only told you that because I wanted in your carrot patch." For spite, he wears his boots to bed that night and his fiancée insists, "If you're going to wear those boots, you get no boot-y!"

In addition to promoting sex prior to marriage, many shows also portray an unrealistic picture of the work relationships require. This is particularly true of shows such as the *The Bachelorette.* Trista meets Ryan and a few weeks later he's down on one knee with a diamond ring in his hand, proposing marriage amid hundreds of flaming candles and fragrant rose petals. Reality television it's called, but it's all set up by television producers, paid for by a television network, and staged for entertainment value. Oh, there was some reality on television during those shows—the commercials for medications that treat herpes, one of the many sexually transmitted diseases, which we'll talk more about in chapter 19.

Television shows can set you up for failure when it comes to guarding your mind, heart, and body from sexual compromise. Magazines are another form of media that may be setting you up for such failure.

MESSAGES FROM TEEN MAGAZINES

CosmoGirl!, YM, and *Seventeen,* just to name a few, whisper messages into your ear about how to be sexy and self-reliant. Page after page of these teen magazines offer a wide variety of tips on how to get good at playing the bad girl.

For example, here are just a few of the articles in the November 2003 issue of *Teen People* magazine:
- "Ready for Moore: Mandy Moore on her guy, her boobs, and her desire not to be a superstar"
- "Sexy A to Z: The scintillating scoop on all things, well, sexy"
- "Dating Diaries: You tried to unleash your inner vixen, but your boy-magnet moves need fixing"
- "Quiz: How Sexy Are You? Find out if you're on fire—or need a light"

- "Special: *Teen People* Sex Survey: What you're really doing when the lights are dimmed—and why"[1]

Unfortunately, many girls look to these magazines far more than they look to the Bible for advice on life, fashion, and relationships. That's why we were thrilled when we saw *Revolve,* a New Testament Bible in glossy, teen-girl magazine form, complete with articles, questionnaires, and advice columns. Here are some of the headlines from *Revolve:*

- "Are You Dating a Godly Guy?"
- "Beauty Secrets You've Never Heard Before"
- "100+ Ways to Apply Your Faith"
- "Guys Speak Out on Tons of Important Issues"[2]

Our daughters and their friends love it and have enjoyed reading *Revolve* not just in their quiet times, but also on road trips and while just hanging out in their rooms.

In addition to television and magazines, music also has a profound impact on young women's sexual values.

MESSAGES FROM THE MUSIC INDUSTRY

Several years ago I met with a sixteen-year-old at her mother's request. My conversation with Melody included what kind of music she listens to, what clothes she wears, and what she fights with her mom about most. Melody claimed her biggest battle was getting her mom to give her money to buy clothes she really loves instead of wasting her money on clothes she'll never wear. "I just like to dress sexy. That doesn't make me a slut or anything," she reasoned.

When I asked what makes her want to dress in such a way, Melody told me about her fascination with Madonna's music and how Madonna's clothes really "rocked." On Melody's dresser was a copy of *People* magazine with Madonna's face framed by pictures of many male celebrities such as Sean Penn, Dennis Rodman, and Michael Jackson. The headline read, "Madonna's Men: Who she loved, who she scared, who she called 30 times in an hour."

Curious about this rock star who has been influencing young women since I was a teenager, I turned to the article entitled "Woman in Love" and read how boy toys came easy for Madonna, who often uses men as "arm candy." Despite her many affairs (some with married men or lesbian lovers) and two abortions because "it just wasn't the right time to have a baby," the article claimed that Madonna is a role model to many women.

> While researching his new biography *Madonna* in Manhattan last winter, Andrew Morton encountered a fan whose feelings for the 43-year-old pop icon went well beyond star worship. [Morton recalls,] "She told me, 'Whenever I have a problem, I think, *What would Madonna do?*'"[3]

Can't you just picture the bracelets and key chains now? WWMD? *What Would Madonna Do?* Now *that* is a scary thought! To *People's* credit, the next paragraph read:

> Judging from Morton's book. . . fans might think twice before following her lead—at least when it comes to love.… [Morton] portrays [Madonna] as an insecure manipulator so desperate for affection that she scared off some boyfriends, two-timed most of them, and almost always made foolish choices.[4]

Please understand that we do not have a stone to throw at Madonna or at Melody. If someone wrote a biographical account of all of our foolish choices, it would not be a pretty picture either. We just pray that Madonna and Melody discover the God who can satisfy their thirst for genuine love, because it can't be found in multiple love affairs, a rockin' wardrobe, chart-topping hit songs, worldwide fame, or vast fortunes.

The same *People* magazine pictures Britney Spears sprawled out across a mattress in low-rise jeans, a white leather sports bra, a belly-button ring, and enough mascara to pave a small parking lot. Previously a member of The Mickey Mouse Club, Britney quickly became one of the most popular young stars, with her face decorating everything from T-shirts to spiral notebooks to lunch boxes. However, as writer Chuck Arnold points out, Mickey Mouse must be covering his ears in horror when Britney sings songs such as "I'm a Slave 4 U," "Lonely," "Boys," "Anticipating," and "Bombastic Love."[5]

As shocking as this erotic picture of Britney is, even more shocking is the silver cross dangling around her neck in the photo. While Britney should be able to display whatever belief in Jesus she may have, young Christian fans who see a cross around her neck may assume that her behavior is okay for a believer. Not.

Unfortunately, the music industry glamorizes female pop stars who have what they consider to be the right look, the right moves, and the right wardrobe. Many of these women set a poor example of biblical concepts of modesty, sexual propriety, and guarding your mind, heart, and body. Before you make an idol out of any pop star, examine her songs and weigh her words against the Word of God. Do you really want those messages to enter your mind?

How to Master the Media

We could go on and on about the sexual messages you can be exposed to through the media, but you get the idea. They are everywhere, so you need to recognize when the world bombards you with bad advice and ungodly examples and learn how to duck and run for cover.

If you want to become a woman of sexual and emotional integrity, we recommend that you take the following steps:

1. Think about all the types of media you enjoy—list the magazines, books, movies, and television shows you watch as well as your favorite songs and musicians. Also include any Web sites that you frequent.
2. Ask yourself the following questions about each item on your list.
   - Would I feel embarrassed if my Christian friends, my pastor, or my parents knew I was indulging in this? Do I feel the need to keep this a secret from them?
   - Does this glamorize ideas, values, or situations that oppose my Christian beliefs?
   - Does this book, show, song, movie or Web site leave me feeling depressed or dissatisfied with myself or hungry for unhealthy relationships?

If you answer yes to any of those questions, it may be a warning that you are on an unwise path.

3. Finally, go to God in prayer about it and ask some WWJD questions:
   - What would Jesus do?
   - What would Jesus spend His time watching?
   - What would Jesus listen to?
   - What would Jesus spend time reading?

Again, one of the primary ways to guard your thoughts is by limiting the access of inappropriate fantasies and images of sexual misconduct to your mind. Closely monitor your reading, viewing, and listening habits. It may seem difficult at first, but it will eventually become second nature.

How I Run for Cover

The following is a list of personal convictions I have about what I look at and listen to, along with explanations of why I've made these choices. These convictions help me run for cover in a compromising, chaotic world and give me freedom to enjoy life without subjecting myself to temptations that might prove overwhelming. I hope they will further spur your thinking about the ways you can guard your mind against temptation.

- *I avoid sexually suggestive television shows.* These shows may provide a few raunchy laughs, but the messages and themes do not benefit me in any way and waste my time. Scripture prohibits the graphic scenarios on these shows, as they usually involve sex outside of marriage (see Matthew 6:22-23). If there is a television show that I know will be uplifting and whole-some, I'll sit down to watch it. But once it's over, so is my viewing time. I get up and move on to something more productive and beneficial. I'd rather spend those prime-time hours tending to my prime relationships—spending time with my family and friends.

- *I don't listen to music that evokes unhealthy sexual cravings or speaks of people in sexually degrading ways.* These are the kind of songs that I listened to growing up, and I'm sure that they had a major impact on my poor sexual choices. As a matter of fact, I can remember sexually suggestive pop, rock, and country songs from the 1980s that shaped me as a person (and not in a good way). Now the last thing I want to do is to listen to songs that stimulate my sexual longings. I listen only to music that isn't offensive to my Christian sexual values.

- *I'm also very selective about the women's magazines I read.* Many of the messages in them aren't helpful to me. When I read pages and pages of advice on how to be thinner and look at the skinny models in their underwear, I can feel dissatisfied and unhappy with my own body. After looking at all of the tight abdomens scattered throughout a magazine, I can get discouraged just looking in a mirror. But when I avoid comparing myself to models and appreciate the strong, healthy body God gave me, I feel much better.

Remember, if you fill your mind with images of sexually compromising comments and situations, you will become desensitized to similar scenarios in your own life. If you guard your mind from these messages, you'll also be guarding your heart and life as well.

THE THIRTY-DAY CHALLENGE

Here's a challenge for you: Turn off your television and resist all worldly sexual messages through movies, magazines, music, the Internet, and so on for thirty days. It's okay to watch the news or something you know is squeaky clean, but if there is any question in your mind as to whether something is appropriate or not, resist it altogether for thirty days. In doing so, you will be giving your mind a break from the media's constant bombardment of sexual messages. By resisting them altogether, you will become "sensitized" to them once again and better able to recognize when the media is feeding you garbage.

Many who have accepted this challenge have reported, "I *can't* watch most television shows or listen to offensive music anymore. It makes me so mad to see how they insult my intelligence and degrade sexuality!" Then they encourage their friends to take the same challenge.

Will you take the challenge? Spend those thirty days enjoying only media and entertainment that supports Christian values. Pray and ask God to help you see and hear things as He does. Then you'll be a true master of your media world!

As you exercise caution, use wisdom, and become a master of the media and its influences in your life, your mind will become free of the negative and degrading messages that can erode your character and endanger your ability to win the battle for sexual and emotional integrity. You'll discover that filtering unhealthy sexual messages from your life is a small price to pay for such enormous and rich rewards.

"I the Lord search the heart and examine the mind, to reward a [woman] according to [her] conduct, according to what [her] deeds deserve."

Jeremiah 17:10

guarding your heart

winning the emotional battle

Above all else, guard your heart, for it is the wellspring of life.

PROVERBS 4:23

When we hear people say, "Girls don't struggle with sexual issues like guys do!" we cannot help but wonder what planet they are from or what rock they have been hiding under. For every young man who falls into sexual sin, isn't there usually a young woman falling with him? Perhaps what these people really mean to say is, "Young women don't struggle with the *physical* aspect of sexuality like a young man does."

Remember, guys and girls struggle in different ways when it comes to their sexuality. A young man must guard his eyes to maintain sexual integrity, but because God made you to be emotionally stimulated, you must closely guard your heart. Your battle is for sexual *and* emotional integrity because if you fail to guard your heart, your body will be much more vulnerable to physical temptations.

Because you are female, your heart naturally longs for attention and affection from the opposite sex. (If your heart longs for affection from other women, please read the afterword.) However, just because you're attracted to someone doesn't mean he is a good match for you, regardless of how good his attention and affection makes you feel.

LOOKING FOR LOVE

Everyone longs to feel loved, and there's nothing sinful about this desire. The problem lies in where we look for love. If you are not getting the love you need from appropriate places, such as your family or healthy friendships, you may go searching for it with reckless abandon. But God has a better way. You don't have to put your heart and body in jeopardy just because you want to be loved. You can seek loving, healthy relationships *and* guard your heart from compromise at the same time. In this chapter and the three immediately following, you will discover

- what God says about the heart and why you need to guard it;
- how to pace yourself emotionally in healthy relationships;
- how to identify when you are about to fall into an inappropriate relationship and what to do about it; and
- where to discover the love your heart yearns for.

GETTING TO THE HEART OF THE MATTER

God tells us to guard our hearts above all else—above our lives, our faith, our relationships, our purses, our dreams, or whatever else we hold dear. As the scripture at the opening of this chapter states: "Above all else, guard your heart, for it is the wellspring of life" (Proverbs 4:23).

Why is this important to God?

The answer is in the word *wellspring,* which can also be interpreted as "source." The heart is the source of life. When God created us, He made our hearts central to our being—physically, spiritually, and emotionally. Physically, the heart is at the center of the circulatory system. It pumps oxygenated blood throughout the body. If the heart has trouble, the entire body is in danger of losing its life-giving flow of blood. Spiritually, the heart is the place that the Holy Spirit dwells when we invite Him into our life (see Ephesians 3:16-17). Emotionally, the heart leaps for joy when we delight in something or someone. It also aches when we experience disappointment or loss. The heart is the core of all we are and experience in life, so when God says to guard it above all else, He is saying, "Protect the source of your life— the physical, spiritual, and emotional source of your well-being."

Just as a lake will not be pure if its source is not pure, neither will your thoughts, words, and actions be pure if your heart is not pure. Eugene Peterson puts it in easy-to-understand terms in *The Message,* which is his paraphrase of the Bible:

> You know the next commandment pretty well, too: "Don't go to bed with another's spouse." But don't think you've preserved your virtue simply by

staying out of bed. Your heart can be corrupted by lust even quicker than your body. Those leering looks [or thoughts] you think nobody notices—they also corrupt. (Matthew 5:27-28)

So if you want to be a young woman of sexual and emotional integrity, be wise about the direction you allow your heart to go. It's one thing to determine how far is too far physically in a premarital relationship, but it's another to answer, "How far is too far *emotionally?*" In order to help you understand where the emotional boundaries are when it comes to your relationships with the opposite sex, please see Figure 15.1.

This model will help you identify the six stages of emotional connection: (1) attention, (2) attraction, (3) affection, (4) attachment, (5) affairs, and (6) addictions. (You will want to refer to this graphic as we address each stage.) While God intends for us to enjoy relationships with the opposite sex, He warns us not to give our hearts to someone who is "forbidden" or who undermines our sexual and emotional integrity. This model can help you recognize where you need to draw the emotional line so you can avoid compromise. Once you learn how to identify the different stages of emotional connection, you can know with confidence where it's okay to go (represented by the green-light level), when to proceed only with great caution

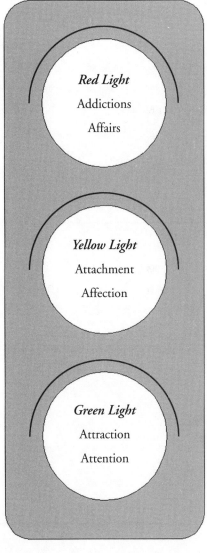

Figure 15.1: Levels of Emotional Connection

(the yellow-light level), and when you must stop and run in the opposite direction (the red-light level).

We encourage you to commit these stages to memory. Before you read the next three chapters, pray and ask God to help you clearly understand these stages and how they can help you guard your heart. Read them as if you are studying for the biggest exam of your entire life. Your understanding, embracing, and applying this information could determine whether you pass or fail the emotional tests you'll experience in future relationships.

 I will praise the LORD, who counsels me; even at night my heart instructs me. I have set the LORD always before me. Because he is at my right hand, I will not be shaken. Therefore my heart is glad and my tongue rejoices; my body also will rest secure.

Psalm 16:7-9

good to go!

> My [daughter], pay attention to what I say; listen closely to my words.
> Do not let them out of your sight, keep them within your heart;
> for they are life to those who find them and health to a [woman's]
> whole body.
>
> PROVERBS 4:20-22

We've all had one of those moments when someone catches our eye for whatever reason. Perhaps you notice a gorgeous guitar player in a band, or maybe your best friend's older brother is a real cutie. Perhaps the bag boy who takes your groceries to the car has a stunning smile, and you wonder if there was a double meaning to his parting comment, "Have a nice day. Come back to see us!"

Should you be concerned if you notice that a guy is eye appealing? Have you crossed the line into compromise? Are you failing to guard your heart just because you find someone handsome? Absolutely not. You have done nothing that goes against Scripture or broken any vows, and any guilt you may be feeling is false guilt. You can rest easy in the fact that your eyes function very well, and you can simply thank God that He makes such fine art.

We want you to be free of any false guilt that you may feel just because a guy catches your eye, so in this chapter we'll talk about the green-light levels of emotional connection, beginning with attention.

WHEN HE GETS YOUR ATTENTION

Sara was a senior in college when she saw an incredibly gorgeous man enter the campus library. She matter-of-factly exclaimed to her friend, "Oh, wow! I'm looking at my future husband!" to which an older woman standing nearby responded, "Sorry, dear, but that's *my* husband!" Needless to say, Sara turned several shades of red with embarrassment—but she had no reason to feel guilty.

When you notice a good-looking guy, he has your attention. This is perfectly healthy, normal, and appropriate, even when he is someone you have no business dating or getting close to. As long as your level of emotional connection doesn't move into the yellow- or red-light stage, you have absolutely no reason to feel guilty.

Many young women ask us, "Will I ever get to the point that I don't notice cute guys anymore than I notice anyone else?" While your awareness of the opposite sex will likely lessen with time and maturity, it will never go away completely. Remember, the desire for love, attention, affection, and relational connection is part of the human condition. It doesn't change because you graduate from high school, because you put a wedding band on your finger, because you have kids, or because you grow old and develop wrinkles and gray hair. The day you stop desiring those things is the day you die. On that day you graduate from the battlefield to the banquet table. There you will feast in the company of Jesus where finally your "soul will be satisfied as with the richest of foods" (Psalm 63:5).

Before we move on to the next stage, we want to dispel a common myth about the attention stage.

COULD IT BE LOVE?

Maybe you've locked eyes with a guy and wondered, *Could this be love at first sight?* No, it's not.

There's no such thing as love at first sight, only attention at first sight. Love isn't an exhilarating feeling, it's a serious commitment that you make after getting to know a person through an extended investment of time and energy. While he may have captured your attention, he has yet to capture your heart. That can be done only over time and with your permission.

Attention is based on what you *see,* and while you may lay eyes on what you consider to be a fine male specimen, that's no guarantee you'll actually be attracted to that person. Attention progresses to attraction only as a result of multiple conversations where you get to know the person more fully.

Let us give you an example to prove our point. Maybe you've noticed a cute guy, only to hear him open his mouth and yell at his sister or brag about his car or complain about someone or something in a nasty way. Did you find yourself attracted to him? Hardly. Regardless of how gorgeous he may be, you probably found yourself turned off. He got your attention, but you felt no attraction. On the other hand, you could meet a very ordinary-looking guy and pay little attention to him but then feel attracted once you get to know him. This is because as a female, you are more stimulated by what you hear than by what you see.

Now for the second stage of emotional connection—attraction. (Please see Figure 15.1 on page 137.)

WHEN ATTENTION BECOMES ATTRACTION

Attention becomes attraction when you get to know a guy well enough to discover that you really like him. Again, there's nothing sinful about feeling attracted to any guy. However, attraction doesn't necessarily give you a green light to date or get close to him.

Despite the messages you receive from the media, being attracted to someone doesn't mean you have to do anything about your attraction. If you are attracted to a particular male friend, don't assume you're going to wind up fooling around with him someday and so attempt to sexualize the relationship. You are *not* powerless over your emotions. You are not "destined" to be with him or to have sex with him, as if you could do nothing to stop it. In fact, you can ignore him altogether if you so choose, whether you do so because the age difference is too great or because he doesn't share your interests and values or because something about him makes the relationship forbidden. (Forbidden relationships are discussed more in chapter 18). You can feel an attraction to him *and* continue to guard your heart and body from sexual compromise by not acting on that attraction in inappropriate ways.

While it's not hard to understand why some people get our attention and others don't, it can be more difficult to understand why we are attracted to some people and not to others. The reasons vary from person to person, and are often based on our experiences growing up.

For example, I once felt a strong attraction to a male family friend. I couldn't understand why until I learned about imago therapy, which teaches that certain people simply "fit your mold" and each person's mold is different. That is why you may have heard a friend rant and rave over her new boyfriend, but you thought after you met him, *What on earth does she see in him?* He fits her mold. He doesn't fit yours.

As I began to understand more about my own particular mold, I realized that this family friend looked very much like my older brother and acted very much like my father. Of course I found him attractive; he fit my mold. But did I panic, thinking I was going to fall into an emotional or sexual affair with him because I found him so attractive? I might have many years ago out of ignorance, but I've learned that both attention and attraction are part of being human. I simply exercised caution by monitoring my behavior around this man and checking my motives for the things I chose to discuss with him. Because I realized it was my brother and my father that I really missed, I also tried to spend more time investing in better relationships with them.

A Higher Purpose

God gave us these green-light stages of emotional connection—attention and attraction—as gifts to be enjoyed. He gave us eyesight to recognize the beauty of His creation, including the opposite sex. He gave us ears and a mouth and a brain that can process information about other people and help us communicate and connect with others. God wants us to appreciate one another and be drawn to one another in Christian love.

But God also had a higher purpose for placing a hunger for attention and attraction within our hearts. He wants our heads and hearts to turn toward Him. As we take notice of our Lord and invest time in getting to know our awesome Creator, He will reveal Himself to us as our magnificent Lover, draw us into a deeper emotional connection with Him, and stir up a longing for His lavish love to fill our hearts to overflowing. Once we experience Jesus in this way, all other people and relationships soon pale in comparison.

Your love, O LORD, reaches to the heavens, your faithfulness to the skies. Your righteousness is like the mighty mountains, your justice like the great deep.... How priceless is your unfailing love! Both high and low among [women] find refuge in the shadow of your wings. They feast on the abundance of your house; you give them drink from your river of delights.

Psalm 36:5-8

proceeding with caution

So, if you think you are standing firm, be careful that you don't fall!

1 Corinthians 10:12

Did you know that one of the goals of this book is to teach you how to make love with your clothes on? Are you surprised? Embarrassed? Does that make you giggle? You're probably wondering, *Are you serious?* Well, in this context *make love* does not refer to having sex. You can learn healthy ways of expressing affection and making someone special feel loved and deeply cared for.

Though we want you to guard your mind, heart, and body from compromise, we also want you to enjoy healthy friendships with guys, and even healthy dating relationships or courtship, because they can help you prepare for a lifetime commitment. But it's very easy to go too far too fast, and for that reason you need to go slowly and carefully. If you learn to determine whether a particular guy is worthy of your affection and commitment and pace yourself emotionally, you won't form deep emotional bonds too quickly or inappropriately. You'll never be caught wondering, *How could I have let this happen?*

In this chapter we'll focus on the yellow-light level of emotional connection, in which you must exercise great caution. (Please see Figure 15.1 on page 137.) In the first yellow-light stage—affection—you need to know how to appropriately express your feelings for a young man you are friends with and feel an attraction for. In the second yellow-light stage—attachment—you need to discern whether this guy is an appropriate person to give your heart to.

When Attraction Becomes Affection

Once a guy catches your attention, you will more than likely want to get to know him. Once you get to know him, you may find yourself attracted to him. And once you find yourself attracted, guess what? You are more than likely going to want to express your affection toward him in a way that confirms to him that you like him as more than just a friend.

While it's natural to express affection in most relationships, you must use caution in expressing affection to the opposite sex. Knowing when and how to express affection can be really difficult. If you are interested in a romantic relationship, you will want to appear open without appearing desperate, and you'll want to avoid expressing affection in any sort of sexually provocative way.

So when is it appropriate to express affection to a guy you are attracted to? When is it not? How do you know the difference? Where do you draw the line?

While we can't provide a list of dos and don'ts, we can suggest some questions to ask yourself as a way of checking your heart in the matter. Prayerfully ask yourself the following questions before deciding to express affection to a guy you are attracted to:

- How well do I really know this guy? Am I confident enough about his character that I can express affection toward him without later regret?
- What is my motive for making this expression of affection? What is my goal, and is it an appropriate one?
- If I want to express affection just to get him to ask me out, would my dating him be acceptable to my parents (and his)?
- Am I trying to show genuine appreciation for this guy, or do I have a hidden agenda? Am I simply fishing for a compliment to get my own ego fed?
- Is this person unattached? Does he have a girlfriend who would be concerned with how I express affection toward him?
- Could this expression be misinterpreted in such a way that this guy would be confused, tempted, or suspicious of my motives?
- Do I sense he has personal feelings toward me that I do not feel toward him? If so, would signs of affection give him the impression I am interested in more than a friendship, when in fact I am not?
- Is this expression of affection one that I wouldn't mind other people (such as my family, youth pastor, or close friends) knowing about?
- Could this expression of affection be interpreted as seductive, or does it reflect godly character?

If you've asked God to reveal your motives, answered each of these questions honestly, and still see no red flags, then it's likely okay to express your affection to this young man in appropriate ways.

But if any of these questions raise a red flag in your spirit, consider keeping your affectionate expressions to yourself until you have 100 percent confidence you are acting with integrity. Continue to be friendly, but don't show him any special treatment as long as you are undecided about your motives. Pray about it, talk with a mature Christian friend about it if you choose, and continue to check your heart. See if the red flags disappear as you get to know him better, or heed the red flags if you feel an increasing conviction that a relationship with this person wouldn't be wise.

If and when you do have a clean conscience about expressing affection toward a guy that you are interested in dating, what are some appropriate ways to do this? In his book *The Five Love Languages,* Gary Chapman says we can express affection in five "languages": gifts, acts of service, words of affirmation, quality time, and physical touch. Figure 17.2 is based on his model. Check it out for appropriate ways vs. inappropriate ways to express affection toward a guy you are interested in.

You can probably come up with a much longer list on your own. In fact, it may be fun to do so and to get your girlfriends' input as well.

BEFORE YOU COMMIT TO BEING A COUPLE

Remember, just because you feel attraction and affection for someone, it doesn't mean you should become a couple. Such a decision should be made carefully and cautiously. We strongly recommend that you and the guy you are interested in spend as much time as possible in the affection stage before moving to the emotional attachment stage. (Please refer back to Figure 15.1 on page 137.) In the affection stage, you are hanging out together, having fun, and getting to know one another as really good friends without commitment to date one another exclusively. You are merely exploring the possibilities of a future, more serious relationship without jumping in blindly.

While in the affection stage, spend time getting to know his friends and family.

Continue to judge his character so that if and when you do make a decision to be-come an exclusive couple, it will be a decision you can feel good about.

Since the affection stage is still exploratory, we recommend that you go out with this person only on group or double dates, and stick to public places to avoid the temptations that secluding yourselves can bring. If you accept an invitation to go to his house (or invite him to yours), make sure a parent or your roommate is going to be home and remain in the gathering areas, not behind a closed bedroom door. If you live in a dormitory situation, meet him in the common areas, or at the

	APPROPRIATE	INAPPROPRIATE
Gifts	• wallet-sized school photo • homemade cookies • note of thanks for helping you	• 8x10 framed glamour shot • lengthy, perfume-scented letter
Acts of Service	• notifying him of a home-work assignment he missed • offering to help shop for his sister's birthday gift	• offering to give a back rub after his football game • helping him wash his car in your swimsuit and short shorts
Words of Affirmation	• complimenting his character • complimenting an article of clothing (such as, "Nice shirt.")	• complimenting how his body looks in an article of clothing (such as, "That shirt makes you look hot.")
Quality Time	• spending time together at the library working on research papers • inviting him to your youth group	• spending every Friday or Saturday night alone together • appearing as Siamese twins in public (never apart)
Physical Touch	• patting him on the back for a good test grade • a high-five in the hallway	• full-body hugs • sitting on his lap • patting his thigh when sitting next to him

Figure 17.2

very least keep the dorm room door propped open to avoid even the appearance of questionable behavior.

While it's fine to let each other know you enjoy and like each other, avoid making long-term promises that you may regret once you get to know him well. Just as a yellow traffic light can quickly turn red, attachments with the wrong person can quickly lead to major relational wrecks!

At this point, in all honesty, love is often blind. You can be so enamored by all the wonderful things you see in him that the bad things fade into the background. That is why it is important to get to know a guy well before you become emotionally attached to him and become a couple. Identify both his strengths and weaknesses before deciding he's a guy you want to commit to and date exclusively.

While emotional attachment is natural and appropriate, it's unwise to emotionally attach to guys over and over, assuming that each boy you go out with must be The One. To understand why, imagine two paper hearts, one red and one black. Apply glue to each and press them together, allowing plenty of time for the glue to dry. Once the two hearts are bonded, pull them apart. What happens? Black fibers remain stuck to the red heart and red fibers still cling to the black. The object lesson is this: When you get attached to someone, you will always keep a part of that person with you, tucking those memories into your trunk of emotional baggage and eventually dragging them into your marriage where you may be tempted to compare your husband to one or all of your previous boyfriends. Also keep in mind that some parts of your heart, once given away, can never be given to someone else, such as first love, first kiss, and first sexual experience.

But that's not the only danger of attaching over and over. Here's another example: Imagine a big strip of clear packing tape. It's sticky, eager to bond with anything it touches. Once attached to a cardboard box, it won't come off without tearing the box and leaving paper residue on the tape. The piece of tape might still be sticky enough to bond to something else, but the more you attach and remove it from other things, the less sticky it becomes. Eventually, it loses its bonding ability altogether.

Something similar can happen with our hearts. When we emotionally attach ourselves over and over to different people, we can lose our emotional "stickiness." So if you continue to have one boyfriend after another after another simply out of

PROCEEDING WITH CAUTION ᷲ 149

habit, you may compromise your ability to remain committed and faithful to one person for a lifetime. When you go from person to person and indulge in a new "flavor of the month" whenever you get a little bored in a relationship, you set yourself up to always crave something new. Then when you find a good guy and settle down, your old patterns of relating can come back to tempt you. As soon as the new wears off your marriage, the craving to sample yet another flavor can be overwhelming.

Just ask Lynette, who has been married four years:

> I remember having different boyfriends throughout junior high and high school, sometimes breaking up with one only to have a new boyfriend before the day was over. One week it was James, the next week Wendel, the next week Chris, then back to James again. I never gave much thought to it back then, but now that I'm married I confess that I often long for the excitement of a new relationship or a rekindled romance with an old flame. It's taken a lot of strength not to just give up when the going gets tough in our marriage and move on to the next interesting guy. A marriage commitment takes a great deal more work than I ever realized while hopping from boyfriend to boyfriend on a weekly basis.

So how can you increase the likelihood that the emotional bond you share with your husband someday will be as strong as possible? By being careful not to emotionally attach to a guy until you have enough evidence to believe that he is a young man of character and a good match for you as a potential mate.

Here are some practical guidelines you can use to decide if it's a good idea for you to date a particular guy exclusively:

- You've known this person as a friend (preferably for at least a year) and are confident about his level of integrity and comfortable with his character.
- You both share a common belief in Jesus Christ as Lord and Savior.
- He has no major character flaws that you eventually want to change (such as drinking or substance abuse, habitual lying, sexual addictions, and so on.)
- You are close to completing your high school education. (It's best to wait until your senior year before getting emotionally involved with one guy).

- You have a sense of what God is calling you to do with your life, and you feel confident that if you eventually decide it's right to marry this person, he would enhance rather than hinder that calling.
- Your college education and/or career plans and goals are complementary to his.
- Your family approves of him and is supportive of your emotional attachment.
- You have invested time getting to know his immediate family, and you feel good about their support of the relationship.

WHEN AFFECTION BECOMES ATTACHMENT

Once you feel confident that the time is right and you've found the right person to become emotionally involved with, your affection will more than likely blossom into emotional attachment, especially if he is as excited about an exclusive romantic relationship as you are. At this point, your heart may begin doing somersaults in your chest. You may daydream about what it might be like to be his wife someday. You may even practice writing your first name along with his last name, just to see how they look together. It is truly an exciting time in a young woman's life when she and that special guy become an official couple.

However, you must continue to judge his character to determine if this is truly the man you want to be with the rest of your life, not just on Friday or Saturday nights. Even though you think you know him well because of the time you have spent checking him out, things can still surface later on in the relationship that are cause for concern. Don't make the mistake, as many girls do when their boyfriends begin to show signs of serious character flaws, of assuming, *Oh, but I have so much invested in this relationship that I can't break it off now.* Even after you've become his girlfriend, if you begin to learn things about him that would keep him from being the kind of husband you deserve someday, bail out now, before you walk down the aisle and get married. The amount of emotional energy a new relationship would require is minimal compared to the tons of emotional energy many women have to spend remaining faithful to a man they wish they'd never married.

You also need to keep your sexual emotions and desires in check, especially being vigilant over your body. Remember, where a woman's heart goes, her body longs to follow. Women often make the mistake of lowering their physical guard during this stage of emotional connection because they are so emotionally stimulated. Many premarital sexual encounters have taken place because, "We just couldn't help ourselves! We're so in love!" Healthy boundaries in committed dating relationships will be discussed further in chapter 22, and in chapter 23 you'll find some guidance for how to decide whether to marry a young man with whom you have emotionally attached. But as you move from the green-light levels to these yellow-light levels of emotional connection, know that time is on your side.

TIME IS YOUR FRIEND

All relationships are absolutely wonderful in the beginning. Tons of guys can thrill you and delight your heart in the first few weeks or months of a relationship. But only time will tell if his love, respect, and commitment to you are genuine. Do yourself a favor and be patient. Just as a rosebud's beauty would be destroyed if it was forced open prematurely, the true beauty of a relationship can't be forced either. You can't rush a healthy romantic relationship. By its very nature, it requires time to blossom into its full, God-given potential.

If women had a dime for every person they were tempted to give their hearts away to, many of us would be filthy rich. However, the wise young woman who takes things slowly, carefully guarding her heart in premarital relationships, will walk down the aisle toward her groom carrying a treasure far greater than riches—a whole heart that is ready to bond with his for a lifetime.

 Lay hold of my words with all your heart; keep my commands and you will live. Get wisdom, get understanding; do not forget my words or swerve from them. Do not forsake wisdom, and she will protect you; love her, and she will watch over you. Wisdom is supreme; therefore get wisdom. Though it cost all you have, get understanding. Esteem her, and she will exalt you; embrace her, and she will honor you. She will set a garland of grace on your head and present you with a crown of splendor.

Proverbs 4:4-9

knowing where to stop!

Do not be misled: "Bad company corrupts good character." Come back to your senses as you ought, and stop sinning; for there are some who are ignorant of God.

1 CORINTHIANS 15:33-34

Have you ever been sitting at a traffic light just when it turns green, only to see another car speed through the intersection even though their light had already turned red? We've seen it happen many times, and we've also seen major collisions as a result of such poor judgment. Maybe the driver thought, *Oh, I'll speed on through the intersection because it would take too much tread off of my tires for me to stop so quickly!* The cost of worn tires is minimal compared to the cost of crumpled cars and crumpled people.

The cost of running emotional red lights is also very high. While we want you to enjoy healthy love relationships, a few relationships are always destructive and unhealthy. You need to guard your heart at all costs against these red-light-level relationships: affairs with "forbidden fruit" and addictions. (Please refer back to Figure 15.1 on page 137.)

AFFAIRS WITH "FORBIDDEN FRUIT"

There are certain romantic relationships a young woman should not entertain under any circumstances, because God clearly forbids them in His Word. Here are some examples of such forbidden fruit:

- non-Christians—"Do not be yoked together with unbelievers" (2 Corinthians 6:14)

- married men—"Marriage should be honored by all, and the marriage bed kept pure, for God will judge the adulterer and all the sexually immoral" (Hebrews 13:4)
- other women—"Homosexuality is absolutely forbidden, for it is an enormous sin" (Leviticus 18:22, TLB)

If you want to guard your heart against compromise, you'll consider these kinds of relationships off-limits. Samantha just wishes she had stopped to consider the cost of involving herself in one such relationship.

When she was a senior in high school, Samantha met Randy at the hospital where she worked. Although he was almost twelve years older than she was and her parents wouldn't have approved, they spent a lot of time together and became close friends. By the time someone told her that Randy was married, she'd already fallen for him. Samantha confesses:

> I wish I could say that I did the right thing and distanced myself from him, but I didn't. He told me he was going through a divorce, and our emotional affair eventually grew into a sexual one after I moved out of my parents' house and began attending college. I tried to justify the affair by the fact that we didn't have intercourse until after his divorce was final. I know even being emotionally involved with a married man was wrong, but that didn't seem to matter much when I was around him.
>
> In my first semester at college, my grades really suffered because of all the time I was spending with Randy instead of studying. I actually had to drop out of a couple of classes to keep from failing them. Then the following semester I was informed that because I wasn't keeping my grades up I lost my scholarship, and now I'm worried that I won't be able to reach my dream of becoming a nurse. If I could rewind the tape of the past year, I'd do a much better job of guarding my heart. I would steer clear of Randy altogether.

Had Samantha guarded her heart, she would have run from this married man and not had to worry about guarding her body—or her grades, or her scholarship, or her career plans.

Perhaps you are attracted to someone who is "forbidden fruit," yet you still wonder how sweet the taste of such a relationship might be. If there isn't such a person now, one will likely cross your path at some point in your life, whether that person is a non-Christian classmate, a married coworker, or your closest female friend. (Lesbian relationships are talked more about in chapter 20 and in the afterword.) Here are some practical questions you can ask yourself to keep your heart in check and make sure you're not in danger of running into the red-light stage of affairs.

- Do I dress to please this person?
- Do I often go out of my way to run into this individual, just to get his (or her) attention?
- Do I spend time with this person every chance I get, neglecting other relationships?
- Do I have to hide my friendship with this person from others?
- Do I look for excuses to call this individual just so I can hear his (or her) voice?
- Do I communicate with this person via e-mail so that others won't know about this friendship?
- Do I obsess over talking or spending time alone with this person, out of earshot or eyesight of anyone else?

If you answered yes to any of these questions, stop and run in the opposite direction from this relationship. Next, pray for God's divine protection, not just over your body, but over your heart, mind, and mouth as well so that you don't do or say anything that would open a door to invite this person into a deeper relationship than is appropriate. Continue to pray anytime you are feeling weak or vulnerable, but make sure this person doesn't become the focus of your prayers. Also pray for your other relationships with family and friends, and if necessary seek their accountability to guard your heart from further compromise. Most importantly, focus on your relationship with God, seeking to grow personally and spiritually and strengthening your resolve against forbidden relationships.

Keep in mind that if you starve your desire to be emotionally intimate with someone, the desire eventually dies. The more you control your appetite for unhealthy relationships, the more dignity and satisfaction you will feel about yourself and your ability to be a young woman of sexual and emotional integrity.

However, if you don't bring your appetite for unhealthy romantic relationships under God's control, you may soon find you're dealing not just with a strong desire for love, but with something much more powerful and difficult to control.

When Love Becomes an Addiction

Webster's dictionary defines an addict as one who "devotes or surrenders oneself to something habitually or obsessively." You can be addicted to anything if you surrender to it without self-control—alcohol, shopping, drugs, and even romantic relationships. As a matter of fact, did you know that romance and sexual activities can be even more addicting than drugs or alcohol?

Gretchen will attest to this. She has three different boyfriends, all unknown to one another. She told us:

> My "public" boyfriend is a basketball player named Tom who goes to my school. He walks me to class, sits with me at lunch, and drives me home when he doesn't have after-school practice. Then there is Ronnie, a guy I met over the Internet. We e-mail each other almost every day. I don't really consider him my boyfriend, but I've never told him about the other guys I am involved with. We flirt and talk about things I wouldn't want the other guys (or anyone else) to know about. Then there's Isaac, who is a freshman on my cousin's college campus. Whenever I go to visit my cousin for the weekend, Isaac is my date to the parties we go to—parties where there is a lot of making out, and Isaac is a great kisser. We write letters occasionally, e-mail each other, and talk on weekends when he has free minutes on his cell phone. I know I'm two-timing (or three-timing!) these guys, but I really like all of them and I can't stand the thought of breaking it off with any of them.

Gretchen doesn't realize she's not just playing with these guys' hearts but also setting herself up for heartache. If you juggle multiple love interests, even as a teenager, you may be putting yourself in a position for future unfaithfulness because you grow accustomed to intensity rather than genuine intimacy. Rather than form deeper emotional bonds with one person, you thrive on the pursuit of the next thrilling moment with the next guy.

What causes a young woman to become addicted to relationships or sex? Doubt or disbelief that God can truly satisfy her innermost needs. When you have this doubt, you may look to a forbidden relationship to satisfy your deep emotional needs, but eventually you'll discover that no one fully satisfies you, no matter how attentive, good-looking, or wonderful that person may be. As you go to the next person, then the next, even allowing some of these relationships to overlap, you are just looking for love in all the wrong places. Romantic relationships are reduced to just "things" that you use to try to fill the vacuum in your heart, but no person ever fills that hole.

God didn't design our hearts to be completely satisfied in human relationships—only in relationship with Him. Once we get filled up with His love, we will be able to love others with integrity. When our relationships are healthy and appropriate, we can respect other people and protect their hearts as well, rather than just using someone to stroke our ego or to get our next emotional fix.

We pray you never experience emotional addictions, and we hope that this book convinces you of your need to create a battle plan to avoid any red-light levels of emotional connection altogether. However, if you've already run this red light, please know there is hope for you. We've known many girls who have journeyed to this depth of desperation, hoping to find something to fill the void in their hearts, only to discover that the pit was far deeper, darker, and lonelier than they could have imagined. I am one of those girls, but after many years of focusing my attentions and affections on my first love, Jesus Christ, my life is a testimony to God's changing grace. In His lavish love, God's arm of mercy reaches farther than we could ever fall.

Because sex and love addictions are beyond the scope of this book, we recommend that you talk with your parents, youth pastor, school counselor, trusted mentor, or even a professional counselor if desperation for sex, love, romance, or relationships controls your life. Ask for help. You will need it if you want to be set free from this destructive pattern and to heal from the wounds that both caused and resulted from this damaging pattern. You don't have to suffer in silence. We also suggest that you pick up a copy of Steve's book *Addicted to Love,* which can help you overcome romance, relationship, and sexual addictions.

THE REWARDS OF WISDOM

Perhaps in the past you have felt that guarding your heart was a gray issue and that it's impossible for a young woman to know how to keep her heart in check. Hopefully, these past few chapters have helped you colorize this issue of emotional integrity with green-, yellow-, and red-light levels so you can identify when you are good to go, when you need to proceed with caution, and when you need to stop altogether before you crash. With this new understanding of emotional integrity, you'll be better able to avoid confusion, false guilt, premature emotional attachment, forbidden relationships, and so on. But best of all, when God sees you are guarding your heart, He will reward you with an even greater revelation of Himself and His extravagant love for you.

 Blessed are the pure in heart, for they will see God.

Matthew 5:8

PART VI

guarding
your body

winning the physical battle

Therefore do not let sin reign in your mortal body so that you obey its evil desires. Do not offer the parts of your body to sin, as instruments of wickedness, but rather offer yourselves to God, as those who have been brought from death to life; and offer the parts of your body to him as instruments of righteousness.

ROMANS 6:12-13

When I graduated from high school, I wanted to become a pathologist and perform surgery on dead bodies to determine the cause of death. However, I couldn't afford medical school, so I decided to do what I considered the next best thing and enrolled in mortuary college!

While in school, I worked at one of the largest funeral homes in Dallas, which actually did the embalming for thirteen other funeral homes in the area. While the majority of bodies I worked on were what you'd expect, elderly people whose time had naturally come to an end, I was shocked at how many people in their teens or twenties came into my embalming room. The usual cause of death in these cases? Either complications from AIDS or suicide as a result of being diagnosed HIV positive. It didn't take a rocket scientist to figure out that these people had met with an early death due to the sexual choices they had made, and in light of how promiscuous I'd been, I couldn't help but think, *It's only by the grace of God that I'm standing over this embalming table instead of lying on top of it.*

A few years later, after I was married and had my first baby, I went to a slide presentation about sexually transmitted diseases and their effects on a woman's reproductive system. I knew plenty about HIV and AIDS, but I was stunned at how many other diseases there were—herpes, chlamydia, gonorrhea, syphilis, human papillomavirus, and many others that are just as difficult to pronounce. I sat there in tears, looking at slides of infected genitals and listening to stories of young women who had contracted a sexually transmitted disease. Many of these patients were unable to have their own children because of the irreversible damage. I wanted to run home, scoop my baby girl up in my arms, and thank God a million times that He had changed my life before I had contracted one of these diseases and blown my chances of ever having my own children.

I asked God, "Why did I not die of AIDS? Why didn't I contract a disease that left me infertile? Why did You spare me? And how can I show my deep gratitude for Your mercy?" In my heart, I clearly heard God say, *My people are destroyed from lack of knowledge [Hosea 4:6]. I want you to give others this knowledge to keep them from perishing.*

Do you want to live to walk down the aisle at your wedding someday? to hold your own babies in your arms after giving birth? to see your children grow up and make you a grandma? to grow old with your husband? If so, please pay close attention as we examine the possible consequences of losing the physical battle for sexual purity. We'll focus on two areas: your own health and the health of your unborn children. But first, let's examine what God says about engaging in any type of sexual act with someone you are not married to, and why.

WHY DOES GOD CARE?

Here are just a few examples of what God says about sexual immorality and fornication, terms that refer to sex outside of marriage.

> Flee from sexual immorality. All other sins a [woman] commits are outside
> [her] body, but [she] who sins sexually sins against [her] own body. Do
> you not know that your body is a temple of the Holy Spirit, who is in you,
> whom you have received from God? You are not your own; you were bought
> at a price. Therefore honor God with your body. (1 Corinthians 6:18-20)

> The acts of the sinful nature are obvious: sexual immorality, impurity and
> debauchery; idolatry and witchcraft; hatred, discord, jealousy, fits of rage,
> selfish ambition, dissensions, factions and envy; drunkenness, orgies, and

the like. I warn you, as I did before, that those who live like this will not inherit the kingdom of God. (Galatians 5:19-21)

Perhaps you've wondered, *What's the big deal about sex outside of marriage? Lots of people do it! Why is this so important to God?*

It's important because He created our bodies, and He designed them to unite with one person—our spouse, in a pure, sexual relationship. He knows that by design, our bodies are physically incapable of fighting off certain germs, bacteria, and diseases transmitted through sexual activity, diseases that will harm us and our ability to fulfill His commandment to "be fruitful and increase in number," which means have sex and make babies! He forbids certain sexual activities, because He wants to help us maintain sexual health and relational happiness.

The bottom line is that God wants the very best for us, and He lovingly communicates to us through Scripture that sex outside of a marriage relationship is not His plan and can be very dangerous. Let's look at why.

WHAT YOU NEED TO KNOW ABOUT YOUR BODY

Before we discuss sexually transmitted diseases, let's look at how God designed the female body to carry a beautiful baby someday (see Figure 19.1 on page 165). Although a woman's genital area consists of many other parts, we are going to limit our discussion to the vital parts of the reproductive system most affected by sexually transmitted diseases: the ovaries, the fallopian tubes, the uterus, the cervix, and the vaginal canal.

- *Ovaries.* Two almond-size organs that house thousands of female reproductive cells called *ova,* or *eggs.* A girl is born with all the eggs she'll ever have, and when she goes through puberty, her ovaries begin releasing one egg each month. This process is called *ovulation.* During sexual intercourse, if one sperm, which is the male's reproductive cell, attaches to this egg, the egg is fertilized and a baby begins to grow.
- *Fallopian tubes.* These two narrow tubes, which connect the ovaries to the uterus, are filled with tiny, hairlike structures called *cilia.* The purpose of

cilia is to sweep the egg away from the ovary and the sperm away from the uterus, drawing them together so that fertilization takes place.

- *Uterus.* Also called the *womb,* this is a baby's home as it is growing and developing for nine months. The uterus is shaped something like an upside-down pear. Each month, the lining of the uterus collects blood in anticipation of a fertilized egg attaching itself and becoming a baby. Until it's born, the baby draws its nourishment from this blood. If no sperm fertilizes the egg, the blood lining gradually exits the body during the menstrual cycle, also referred to as a *period,* which lasts from three to seven days.

- *Cervix.* The cervix is a round muscle separating the uterus from the vaginal canal. Its primary purpose is to contract, closing up and forming a mucous plug when a woman first becomes pregnant. This provides protection for the *amniotic sac,* the fluid-filled sac that the surrounds the baby as it develops. When the baby is ready to be born, the cervix will begin opening, or dilating, and release the mucous plug. When the cervix measures ten centimeters in diameter, it will allow passage of the baby's head and body.

- *Vaginal canal.* This elastic, muscular passageway is approximately three to four inches long when fully developed. If you use tampons during your period, you insert them into your vaginal canal. During the act of sexual intercourse, the penis is inserted into this canal. It is called the *birth canal* because during birth a baby is delivered into the world through this passage.

Now that you know your body a little better, let's take a look at what can happen if you don't protect it by saving sex until marriage.

WHAT YOU NEED TO KNOW ABOUT SEXUALLY TRANSMITTED DISEASES

Until the 1970s, people were aware of only two significant types of diseases that you could get from sexual contact: syphilis and gonorrhea. A shot of penicillin could easily cure both of these diseases, so they weren't much of a deterrent from sexual activity.

Today however, researchers estimate there are between twenty and twenty-five significant types of sexually transmitted diseases (STDs), only a few of which will be discussed here. A panel of experts reported the following statistics on STDs in the United States:

- 15 million new cases of STDs occur each year in Americans.
- Over 68 million people have an STD in the United States.
- STDs cost our country over 8 billion dollars each year.
- Genital herpes currently infects more Americans (45 million) than any other STD.
- Human papillomavirus (HPV) has the highest yearly incidence of new infections (5.5 million).[1]

The STD that usually gets the most attention is HIV (human immunodeficiency virus). It robs the body of its disease-fighting abilities so that it eventually develop AIDS (Acquired Immune Deficiency Syndrome), which compromises the immune system and makes a person susceptible to death from a wide variety of ailments, such as leukemia or pneumonia. AIDS can also be passed through the mother's blood supply to her unborn baby, possibly resulting in that child's death at an early age. It is estimated that over twenty million people have already been killed by AIDS, and that forty-two million people are currently infected with the

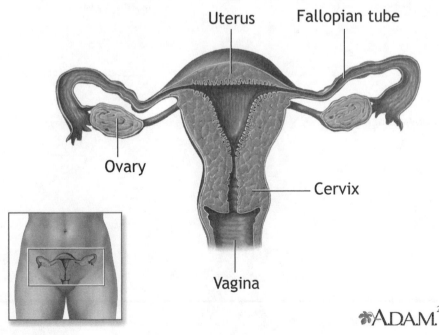

Figure 19.1

disease.³ AIDS prevention efforts are usually aimed at teenagers, because they are far more likely than adults to engage in risky sex practices with multiple partners.

If we weren't hearing so much about HIV, we would hear a lot more about HPV (human papillomavirus). This disease has the highest annual rate of infection (again, 5.5 million people each year in the United States alone). While bacterial infections can be treated with antibiotics, viral infections such as HPV, herpes, and HIV have no cure. Symptoms of viral infections can be treated, but ultimately the virus stays with you for life. Here is what the Medical Institute for Sexual Health (MISH) has to say about HPV:

- HPV is the virus present in over 93 percent of all cases of cervical cancer.
- Each year in the United States, more women die from cancer of the cervix than from AIDS.
- Most Americans, including health care professionals, are currently unaware of how common HPV is. In addition to cervical cancer, HPV can lead to cancer of the vagina, penis, anal canal (via anal sex*), or mouth (via oral sex).
- Dr. Richard Klausner of the National Cancer Institute has stated, "Condoms are ineffective [protection] against HPV because the virus is prevalent not only in mucosal [wet] tissue, but also on dry skin of the surrounding abdomen and groin [the area between your legs], and can migrate [move] from those areas into the vagina and cervix."⁴

HPV can cause warts which doctors often burn off with a laser, sometimes leaving the affected tissue (usually the cervix or the outer vaginal area called the *vulva*) damaged. Often, the cervix muscle will be weakened as a result of such surgery and may not be strong enough to remain closed during pregnancy, increasing the chances of miscarriage.†

EVEN IF YOU DON'T HAVE ANY SYMPTOMS...

Despite all the warnings about STDs, many young people continue having vaginal, anal, or oral sex. They think, *I couldn't possibly have a disease, because I have*

---

* *anal sex*—insertion of the penis into the anal canal rather than the vaginal canal

† *miscarriage*—the accidental loss of a pregnancy due to medical complications

absolutely no symptoms! Or, *I always practice "safe sex," so I don't have to worry about STDs.* Or perhaps they cautiously ask their potential partner, "Do you have any diseases?" to which the person replies, "Oh no!"

Before you assume there's no risk, get this: MISH estimates that 70 to 80 percent of the time, an STD carrier will have absolutely *no symptoms.* Without proper medical testing, you or your partner may never know you have the disease, but you can certainly pass it on to any partner you come in contact with. Even with medical testing, some diseases such as HPV are difficult to detect. Many of these diseases will be your companions for life and will likely cause infection in anyone you have any type of sexual activity with. This includes vaginal sex, oral sex, anal sex, or mutual masturbation.*

Certain segments of society have convinced many people that if you have protected sex, you won't have to fear disease. While using a condom† may make sex more safe than unprotected sex, condoms by no means make sex safe. Dr. Susan Weller says, "It is a disservice to encourage the belief that condoms *will prevent* sexual transmission of HIV."[5] In a study to determine if condoms protect against the spread of HIV, researchers estimate that the true effectiveness of condoms in risk reduction is only 69 percent. With a 31 percent risk factor, using condoms to prevent the spread of HIV is about as dangerous as putting two bullets in a six-chamber gun and playing Russian roulette.‡ Not very smart, huh?

If you truly want to protect yourself, you'll guard against sexual compromise altogether. No condom fully protects you against the possible physical consequences of sex outside of marriage. No condom protects you against the spiritual consequences of sin, which is broken fellowship with God. No condom will protect you from the emotional consequences of a broken heart. As a matter of fact, studies show that once a teenage girl engages in sexual intercourse outside of marriage, she

---

* *mutual masturbation*—touching another person's genitals then touching your own, coming in contact with one another's body fluids
† *condom*—a latex covering for a man's penis that reduces the risk of pregnancy and some STDs
‡ *Russian roulette*—a ridiculously dangerous game in which a person puts one bullet into a six-chamber gun, puts it to his or her head, and pulls the trigger, hoping that the bullet remains in the gun rather than going through his or her brain

becomes three times more likely to commit suicide than a girl who is a virgin.[6] When a girl gives her virginity away, it usually results in low self-esteem, regret, shame, and enormous emotional pain. Therefore, don't think in terms of "safe sex," but in terms of "saving sex" until marriage.

If this revelation comes after you've allowed your physical boundaries to be crossed, do yourself a favor and go to a doctor for an STD screening. We realize it may be difficult or embarrassing, but proper treatment may save your life, the life of your future partner, and the lives of your future babies.

FOR THE SAKE OF YOUR UNBORN CHILDREN

If you are like most of your peers, you want to have kids someday. This desire is one of the most common we as human beings have—to reproduce life and pass on a legacy of love to our offspring. Psalm 127:3-5 says:

> Sons [and daughters] are a heritage from the LORD,
>> children a reward from him.
> Like arrows in the hands of a warrior
>> are sons [and daughters] born in one's youth.
> Blessed is the man [and woman]
>> whose quiver [or house] is full of them.

If you want to have your own children someday, we hope you are studying this book very carefully. Your victory in this battle could very well determine your ability to conceive and bear your own children. You see, some sexually transmitted diseases will cause scar tissue to build up in your fallopian tubes, preventing your eggs from ever uniting with your husband's sperm. You may think, *Yeah, but I'll just go to an infertility clinic, and they can help me get pregnant.* But there's no guarantee that medical procedures will successfully result in pregnancy and a healthy baby, and infertility treatments cost an enormous amount of hard-earned money, precious time, and emotional energy. We have many friends who will testify to this fact.

Also be warned that having an abortion may harm your ability to bear children.

Often when a young woman gets pregnant before she is married, she views abortion as the easy way out. No public shame, no humiliation among her friends and family—just get rid of the baby and no one will ever have to know. But here's a word of wisdom from Deborah, a woman who wants you to learn from her mistake instead of making your own:

> When I was nineteen, I chose to have an abortion when my boyfriend
> refused to marry me or help take care of the baby. I thought it was the easy
> way to bring a quick end to a big mistake. But I can't describe the shame and
> intense pain I have felt over the past twenty years, especially at Christmas
> and also in April, when we would have been celebrating his or her birthday.
> The abortion left me with permanent damage to my uterus, and I was never
> able to have my own baby, even after marrying a good man who wanted to
> father a child. How I wish I had chosen to live with the humiliation of an
> unplanned pregnancy for nine months and then placed the baby in a loving
> adoptive home. That would have been much easier than carrying the burden
> of murdering my own child and becoming infertile. It's a regret that I'll take
> to my grave.

In an article entitled "Failed Promises of Abortion," Maggie Gallagher says that one out of four babies will be killed before birth due to abortion. She also had this to say:

> What abortion does deliver for women is the ability to routinely engage in
> the sexual practices of the worst kind: meaningless sex with uncommitted
> partners.... The irony for women is that these risky sexual practices are not
> even enjoyable. For women, recent research confirms, sexual satisfaction
> depends primarily on the emotional quality of her relationship with the
> man she is letting inside her body.[7]

Maggie is right. Sex outside of a committed marriage relationship may be a physical temptation, but those who have experienced premarital sex can testify that it doesn't satisfy a woman's innermost desire for love, intimacy, and security. Only sex by God's design with a loving, faithful, committed marriage partner can do that.

ARE YOU READY FOR VICTORY?

Now that you know more than you ever wanted to about sexually transmitted diseases and have a clearer understanding of why God's plan for sex is only inside marriage, are you ready to construct a surefire line of defense against STDs, unplanned pregnancy, and infertility? Good!

In the next three chapters we'll examine some specific ways to guard your body against sexual compromise. Keep reading!

 Do not be deceived: God cannot be mocked. A [woman] reaps what [she] sows. The one who sows to please [her] sinful nature, from that nature will reap destruction; the one who sows to please the Spirit, from the Spirit will reap eternal life.

Galatians 6:7-8

"technical" virginity

The body is not meant for sexual immorality, but for the Lord, and the Lord for the body.

1 CORINTHIANS 6:13

I had looked forward to this night for several weeks, and it finally arrived—a very special date to a new, exciting place with a very special person. We drove into the parking lot of the brand-new stadium for a Texas Rangers baseball game, just me and my niece, out for her tenth birthday celebration. Our conversations in the car had been lighthearted and filled with laughter. Then I said, "Paige, now that you are ten, I know that you might have some questions once in a while that you don't know who to turn to for answers. I just want you to know that you can ask me anything you want, anytime you want." Little did I know what I was getting myself into when Paige responded, "Aunt Shannon, what is oral sex?"

I expected questions about hairstyles or school or maybe boys. But oral sex? Coming from a ten-year-old, that one caught me off guard, to say the least. I asked her where she'd heard about oral sex, to which she responded, "I hear it all the time on the radio!"

In 1998, just when you were likely formulating your opinions and ideas about sex and sexuality, our nation was bombarded with media coverage of the White House sex scandal. Former president Bill Clinton insisted that he had not lied about having sexual relations with Monica Lewinski, because, as he basically said, oral sex is not sexual relations. While his accusers didn't buy into this argument, unfortunately many young people did.

Consider these statistics:

- According to a fall 1999 survey conducted by *Seventeen* magazine, of the 723 male and female teens (ages fifteen to nineteen) who were approached in malls, 49 percent considered oral sex to be "not as big a deal as sexual intercourse," and 40 percent said it did not count as "sex."[1]

- A recent survey of fifteen- to nineteen-year-old girls and boys found that 55 percent reported having engaged in oral sex.[2]
- A Manhattan psychologist was quoted as saying that oral sex is "like a goodnight kiss" to many adolescents in a description of how seventh- and eighth-grade virgins who were saving themselves for marriage were having oral sex in the meantime because they perceived it to be safe and risk-free.[3]

WHAT'S BEHIND THE "ORAL SEX ISN'T SEX" MYTH?

It's often been said lately that oral sex has become the "sex of choice" among teens and young adults, usually with girls on the "giving" end rather than on the "receiving" end. Why has oral sex become so popular?

Believe it or not, many young women see oral sex as the ultimate bargain. Why? Here are several reasons, along with our response:

- *There's no risk of pregnancy.* However, because sexual passion escalates so quickly, many young people engage in sexual intercourse shortly after experimenting with oral sex. Then possible pregnancy *does* become an issue.
- *I can't get an STD from oral sex.* If this is what you think you'd better think again! Human papillomavirus, herpes simplex virus, and hepatitis B are some of the viral STDs that can be transmitted orally,[4] while gonorrhea, syphilis, chlamydia and chancroid are some of the bacterial infections that can be passed through oral sex.[5] Maybe you think having one of these diseases in your mouth isn't as bad as having it in your vaginal area, but when you get an STD in your mouth from oral sex, you could give it to someone else just by kissing, then he could pass it on to your vaginal area if he has oral sex with you. As we mentioned in the last chapter, vaginal penetration doesn't have to take place in order for you to get an STD.
- *I can be more popular with guys.* But who wants to be popular because you're an easy target for oral sex? You may get guys' attention by performing sexual favors, but no way will you get their respect, unconditional love, or commitment.

- *I want to "make him happy."* If a guy tells you that oral sex is the way to make him happy, he's not *loving* you at all. He's *using* you, and you need to run from that relationship at breakneck speed. If it is *your* idea and desire to perform oral sex to make him happy, we recommend you run to the nearest professional counselor at your church or school to sort through this issue before you begin doing things you'll regret. Such sexual choices can easily progress into habits and, eventually, sexual addictions.
- *I have control over him* (whereas with sexual intercourse, the guy is perceived as having the control). Because many young women have been sexually abused and coerced into performing sexual acts that they didn't want to do, the illusion of maintaining power over a guy during oral sex can be an appealing one. But such control is a figment of your imagination. If performing oral sex is your idea, you may control him for all of two minutes, but once ejaculation* takes place and he gets his sexual release, you just lost your control over him. If oral sex is his idea and you allow yourself to be coerced into doing this, he's controlling you, not vice versa.

As you take all these things into consideration, we hope you'll agree that oral sex outside of marriage *is,* in fact, sexual activity that you should refrain from altogether as a young woman of sexual and emotional integrity.

OTHER MISCONCEPTIONS ABOUT ABSTINENCE

Oral sex isn't the only activity that many mistakenly associate with a sexually abstinent lifestyle. One study revealed that 61 percent of college freshmen and sophomores considered mutual masturbation to be abstinent behavior and that 24 percent thought anal sex was abstinence as well.[6] The philosophy seems to be that "if I can't get pregnant by doing it, it's abstinence!" This is an extremely limited and false view of sexual abstinence. A sexually abstinent lifestyle means refraining from any type of genital contact or any other activity which serves to arouse you (or him) sexually. Oral sex, mutual masturbation, and anal sex all fall into that category and should be avoided altogether.

---

* *ejaculation*—the height of a male's sexual pleasure when semen suddenly emits from his penis

Many believe these behaviors are acceptable, and think, *As long as there is no vaginal penetration, I'm abstinent and, therefore, still a virgin.* A "technical" virgin perhaps, but still a virgin. So, in her mind, performing oral sex for a guy isn't really sex. Allowing him to perform oral sex on her isn't really sex. Allowing him to touch her vaginal area or even penetrate her vaginal canal with his fingers isn't really sex. Giving him a "hand job" isn't really sex. In the technical virgin's mind, she can still call herself sexually pure as long as no penis has ever been inserted into her vagina.

We don't want to rain on anyone's purity parade, but being merely a technical virgin is nothing to be proud of. It basically just says that you are unable to exercise sexual self-control and are barely hanging on to your virginity by one single thread—the thread of vaginal penetration.

If you've already engaged in some of these activities, please do not feel condemned; God does not condemn you (see Romans 8:1). God's people are destroyed from lack of knowledge. My coauthor and I want to give you information that will help you live with sexual purity and integrity. We have both previously made some very unwise sexual choices out of ignorance, and we want to equip you with all of the information that we wish we had when we were your age to keep you from making similar mistakes. We want you to find the joy we have found in freedom and obedience.

We want to help you understand why your complete abstinence is so important to God, but before we do, let's address one other current misconception about abstinence.

THE LURE OF LESBIAN EXPERIMENTATION

Many young women today falsely assume that lesbian* experimentation is no big deal. They think, *I'll just experiment with girls, but it's not really sex.* Again, this goes back to "as long as there's no vaginal penetration, I'm not having sex," and since lesbian lovers don't have a penis, girls think they can experiment with each other and still be virgins. Some assume that lesbian experimentation is a perfectly normal

---

* *lesbian*—relating to homosexuality between females

part of discovering your true sexual identity. *How will I know if I'm gay or straight if I don't try both?* they reason. Others fool around with same-sex partners because it has become a relatively popular thing to do. Some, even as early as middle school, just like the shock value when they boldly declare, "I'm bisexual!" Others hook up with other girls because they believe guys will think it's cool and be more interested in them.

Lesbian experimentation is *not* an acceptable form of abstinence. Such goes directly against Scripture (see Leviticus 18:22; Romans 1:24-26) and fuels sexual passions and curiosities to the point that "just playing around" sexually with another female can become addictive, creating an enormous amount of confusion, guilt, and turmoil in your life.

> "I want to marry a girl who has saved herself for me just as I am saving myself for her. I want her to be concerned not just with her physical virginity, but with her complete purity."
>
> —DANNY

Just ask Mary. Even though she's been a Christian for eleven years, wants to live a life pleasing to God, and has always desired a healthy, pure relationship with a man someday, lesbian experimentation has led her to a place that she never wanted to go. Mary shares her story:

> I am seriously struggling with the sexual relationship with a female friend in my life. I never considered myself a lesbian, but she and I began fooling around with each other, and our relationship became very sexual. I know God wants me to stop this, but it's so hard. I keep falling back into this, and I don't know where to go from here.

We're sure Mary wishes she'd never gone there in the first place. Sin is much easier to resist in the beginning. Once we taste forbidden fruit, we often develop an appetite for it. If you have involved yourself in lesbian experimentation and find that you cannot break free, we urge you to see a counselor before this becomes an all-consuming lifestyle that robs you of a happy marriage and a rich, fulfilling life someday.

Before we move on, allow us to clarify the difference between child sexual play and lesbian experimentation. Some of you may be reading through this and thinking, *Yikes! What about the things that Suzie and I did when we were five!* Most young children go through a season of sexual curiosity and engage in sexual behaviors, such as "playing doctor" or "playing husband and wife," sometimes with a boy partner, but often with a girl partner, especially if you frequently had a girl or perhaps a female cousin spend the night.

Know that the sexual activities you engaged in as a young child did not make you a lesbian and are not cause for alarm. What we are warning against is the deliberate decision to engage in sexual behaviors beyond the age of accountability. If you are old enough to be reading this book, you are old enough to monitor your own sexual behaviors and make choices that truly support an abstinent lifestyle. Hopefully by reading this, you will be not only convicted to do so, but also equipped and excited about doing so.

WHY IS MY ABSTINENCE SO IMPORTANT TO GOD?

We don't want to leave you with the impression that God just creates these long lists of rules to make things hard for you, boss you around, or rob you of your fun. Your complete abstinence from all sexual activity, not just intercourse, is so vitally important to Him because your purity and holiness are top priority to Him. Why? Because it is only through purity and holiness that we discover the overcoming, abundant life of freedom from sin and ultimate joy that God desires for us. Remember, He loves us so much more than we could imagine—even more than we love ourselves. He wants you to avoid trying to get around the "no sex until marriage" rule for five reasons:

1. *Perfect physical health.* He made your body, and He knows it is susceptible to germs and diseases that could rob you of your perfect sexual health and ability to have your own children someday. He made you to be healthy and to "be fruitful and increase in number" (Genesis 1:22), and abstinence will greatly increase your ability to do so.

2. *Perfect mental health.* He wants you to be free from the temptations and fantasies that overwhelm people's minds when they begin dabbling in sexual immorality. He wants you to think clearly and use good judgment.

3. *Perfect emotional health.* He wants to protect you from a broken heart, from guilt, and from low self-esteem. He doesn't want you to be plagued by depression but filled with joy unspeakable.

4. *Perfect spiritual health.* He wants you to feel complete freedom to enter into His presence and enjoy fellowship with Him, and He knows that sexual sin will hinder you from experiencing that freedom.

5. *Perfect relational health.* God created your vaginal area to be an incredibly special place, a place where you and your husband can bond together in such a personal, deeply intimate way that your relationship is completely set apart from all others. Your marriage is designed to be sexually exclusive and stronger, more permanent than any other relationship you have ever had. For this reason, God wants you to protect your body, which is a temple of His Holy Spirit, especially that place which would be considered your "holy of holies," the private place within the temple reserved strictly for the most divine purposes. And providing a healthy, wonderful, exclusive place for intimate sexual relations with your husband someday certainly qualifies as a *divine* purpose.

SO WHAT'S THE ANSWER?

If oral sex, mutual masturbation, anal sex, or lesbian experimentation is not the answer to getting around the "no sex until marriage" rule that God has so lovingly created for our safety and well-being, then what *is* the answer? How can you find sexual fulfillment?

As repeated throughout this book, there's only one way to experience ultimate fulfillment, and that's by doing things God's way. There's only one way to avoid the risk of unplanned pregnancy and sexually transmitted diseases. There's only one way to maintain your virginity and genuinely protect your sexual purity. It's the same way that you can make one special guy deliriously happy someday with your sexual favors and prove your ability to remain faithful to him—by exercising self-control so you are not intentionally arousing each other physically. Of course we are not talking about technical virginity but about living a completely abstinent and truly abundant lifestyle.

But the fruit of the Spirit is love, joy, peace, patience, kindness, goodness, faithfulness, gentleness and self-control. Against such things there is no law.

Galatians 5:22-23

sex without strings

It is God's will that you should be sanctified: that you should avoid sexual immorality; that each of you should learn to control his own body in a way that is holy and honorable, not in passionate lust like the heathen, who do not know God.

1 THESSALONIANS 4:3-5

On June 19, 2003, *Good Morning America* reported that 20 percent of teenagers have sex before their fifteenth birthday. In 2001, The Center for Disease Control reported that 45.6 percent of high-school students in the United States have had sexual intercourse.[1] In a newspaper article titled "Abstinence Pledges Not Very Effective," Mary Meehan wrote that "according to a survey of nearly 600 teens, 61 percent of those who had taken abstinence pledges had broken them within a year. Of the 39 percent who said they had not broken their pledges, more than half disclosed they'd engaged in oral sex."[2]

According to the young women we've talked to, most don't grow up with the intention of giving their virginity away prior to marriage, so what happens along the way that causes a young woman to give up this precious gift? Or even if she manages to protect her physical virginity, what causes a young woman to engage in other sexual behaviors, such as oral sex or mutual masturbation? It's likely that not only did she fail to guard her mind and heart, but she didn't guard her body by having safe boundaries in place.

CASUALTIES OF CASUAL SEX

You might imagine that young women give in to a variety of sexual activities because they get so tangled up in a serious, committed relationship and think, *We're going to get married anyway.* But this isn't the reasoning behind many of today's sexual encounters. Since the sexual revolution of the 1970s and '80s, many people have sex with someone they don't have a committed relationship with and even with someone they barely know. Over the past several decades, many have come to view sex as an extracurricular activity, just another pleasurable pastime. Many young women tell us that it's now popular to "hang out and hook up," have "friends with benefits," or be "booty buddies." In other words, sex without any commitment expressed or expected. They meet, they mate, and they walk away to find their next "hookup."

In a *USA Today* article on casual sex, Mary Beth Marklein reported on this trend. In her article she included the following quote, written by Yale University student Natalie Krinsky in the November 1, 2002, column for the *Yale Daily News* called "Sex and the (Elm) City":

> Women know within the first five minutes of meeting a man whether they
> are going to hook up with him or not. But…women don't want the guy to
> know he'll be hooking up until he's actually doing it…. Post hookup is
> when guys tend to get ambiguous [they ignore you]. It's their payback. Do
> they want to hook up again? Dunno. Do they want to date? Dunno. Are
> they straight? Dunno. Name? Dunno.[3]

Don't make the assumption that only non-Christians engage in sex without strings. We know plenty of people who could tell you otherwise, and Kelly is one of them. She had no intention of hooking up with anyone the night she went to a beach party with some friends. But that was before she laid eyes on a gorgeous guy. Kelly says:

> He was everything I had dreamed of—handsome, well-built, and all that.
> I ended up riding home with him that night, and when he invited me in,
> I accepted his invitation. We talked for a couple of minutes and then began
> kissing. Then we started rubbing against one another, bumping and grinding
> our bodies together as if we were having sex with our clothes on. Within
> a matter of minutes, the clothes came off, and I was giving my virginity to

a guy that I had just met a few hours before. I'm not sure why I didn't stop him. It all happened so fast that I really didn't have time to think about it.

As Kelly discovered, a guy who initially rocks your world can also leave it in shambles if you don't have firm physical boundaries in place. Nicole is another young woman we know whose world was left in shambles, not as a result of one relationship but because of many sexual relationships. She admits:

> Since I was fifteen I've had a few relationships here and there, but for the most part I've had "friends with benefits." I liked kissing guys and making out with them, but of course they'd want to have sex, too, so I'd usually go along. I figured I had to give these guys what they wanted if I was going to get what I wanted.
>
> After a while I became addicted to hooking up with guys. Every weekend I would go to a football game or a party and see someone that was attractive and go mess around with him, often giving out oral sex like it was candy or something. I didn't care if I knew him. In fact, it was better if I didn't because then I wouldn't have to worry about awkwardness or strings later on. The problems that came from all of this lack of good judgment is that I've struggled with depression, anger, jealousy, lack of self-confidence, and feelings of worthlessness. I began to hate myself and considered suicide as a way out.

Fortunately, God provided a better way out for both Nicole and Kelly. Each of these women enrolled in a Women at the Well class at Teen Mania (www.teenmania. org) and got to the root of why they've engaged in such unhealthy behaviors. Today, they are living exemplary lives of sexual integrity and are determined to turn their generation around, back toward God and honorable sexual behavior.

A QUICK COLLEGE-PREP COURSE

Be prepared. Casual sex is about as common on most college campuses as textbooks. When you leave your parents' home and go off to college or to live on your own, you will most likely face fierce sexual temptations, and you'd better have some firm boundaries in place!

Boston College student Anna Schleelein vividly paints the picture of the sexual temptations young men and women frequently face in dormitory-style living:

> College is screwed up. It's not real life. They took six thousand of us who are in our sexual prime and crammed us into dorm rooms where there's nowhere to sit except on the bed. Members of the opposite—or same, of course— gender are but a single flight of stairs away, and often right next door.[4]

However, many young people *are* living with integrity, so don't think for a minute that it can't be done. It's simply a matter of guarding your mind and heart and establishing firm physical boundaries. As a matter of fact, living by these boundaries in junior high and high school is the best way to prepare for those tempting college and adult years.

Before we go any further, let's check out what life's best instruction manual has to say about casual sex.

SEARCHING THE SCRIPTURES

How do you think God responds to such behavior as friendships with benefits and sexual hookups? Let's take a long, hard look at several scriptures to get a grip on God's point of view about such sexual activity.

> Therefore God gave them over in the sinful desires of their hearts to sexual impurity for the degrading of their bodies with one another. They exchanged the truth of God for a lie, and worshiped and served created things rather than the Creator....
>
> Because of this, God gave them over to shameful lusts. Even their women exchanged natural relations for unnatural ones. In the same way the men also abandoned natural relations with women and were inflamed with lust for one another. Men committed indecent acts with other men, and received in themselves the due penalty for their perversion. (Romans 1:24-27)

Based on this scripture, it is evident that casual sex is far beyond the realm of what God considers honorable. Notice that God doesn't intervene and say, "Hey, you can't do this!" He gives people the freedom to make their own sexual choices (see verse 24), but those sexual choices also come with consequences (see verse 27). The moral of that story is that if you want healthy consequences, make healthy sexual choices now. Let's take a look at another scripture.

> It is God's will that you should be sanctified: that you should avoid sexual immorality; that each of you should learn to control his own body in a way that is holy and honorable, not in passionate lust like the heathen, who do not know God; and that in this matter no one should wrong his brother or take advantage of him. The Lord will punish men for all such sins, as we have already told you and warned you. For God did not call us to be impure, but to live a holy life. Therefore, he who rejects this instruction does not reject man but God, who gives you his Holy Spirit. (1 Thessalonians 4:3-8)

Did you catch that last part? When we reject God's teaching about avoiding sexual immorality, we reject God Himself. Casual sex flies in the face of God, creating a stench in His nostrils. These are strong words, but we're not going to water down Scripture to make anyone feel better about sexual immorality. It's important you're clear about how God feels about sexual activity outside of marriage (not just intercourse, but all sexually related activities such as oral sex, anal sex, mutual masturbation, and lesbianism) so that you will choose a different course than many of your peers choose. My coauthor and I pray that you will choose to

- establish and maintain healthy, God-honoring physical boundaries;
- live by God's perfect plan of saving sexual intimacy for marriage; and
- enjoy the *best* sex possible—one woman with one man for a lifetime within a marriage relationship.

So what would good boundaries in casual relationships look like? Let's start from the beginning—when you first notice someone, and go from there. Keep in mind that these are physical boundaries for casual relationships, so we'll address friendships here, and boundaries for committed relationships (boyfriend/girlfriend) in the next chapter.

FRIENDS DON'T LET FRIENDS CROSS THE LINE

Once you become more than just acquaintances and consider yourself friends, you may be tempted to cross physical boundary lines that can jeopardize your (or his) ability to maintain good judgment. To prevent this from becoming an issue in your casual relationships, think of the nature of friendship. Friends talk with each other, laugh together, look out for each other, and so on, but friends don't go out of their way to turn each other's heads or turn each other on. Friends care about protecting each other's mind, heart, body, and soul and will make sacrifices to avoid causing each other to stumble and fall into compromising situations.

We often see young women cross the line in the way that they hug their male friends. While you may give a guy a hug around the neck or pat on the back, it's inappropriate to press your breasts against his body and act as if you are going to passionately wrestle him down to the ground. This kind of hug gets guys' sexual juices flowing. Consider sticking to "side hugs," where you come up to guys and pat them on the back while standing side by side. Or perhaps give an "A-frame" hug by reaching forward with your body and embracing the other person's neck with your arms, avoiding the impression that you are trying to press your body completely against his for sexual arousal.

We also see a lot of young women sitting on guys' laps just to be cute or because "there's not enough seats!" Before sitting on a guy's lap, consider this: When you do so, your genital area is directly on top of his genital area, which is very arousing to him, even if it is only "sitting on his lap" to you. Also, your breasts are directly in front of his eyes, and he can't help but notice them. If the room is overly crowded, take a seat on the floor instead of using a guy's lap as your throne. Also refrain from lying horizontally next to a guy sardine-style or draping your legs over him, as this can be very arousing as well. If you want to affectionately touch a guy friend, give him a gentle squeeze on the arm, a pat on the back, or one of those side hugs we just talked about.

Your breasts, hips, buttocks, upper thighs and genital area should be off limits to any kind of touching, grabbing, pinching, slapping, and so on, even in jest. Don't allow anyone to touch any part of your body, whether through your clothes or underneath them, that a modest swimsuit and shorts would normally cover.

You can certainly add to this list of boundaries as a way of guarding your body from sexual compromise with acquaintances and friends. Let wisdom be your guide and always use good judgment. If something doesn't feel right to you, it probably isn't. Trust your instincts and maintain safe distances in your casual relationships. By doing so you'll be protecting yourself and the guys around you, setting an example for your girlfriends, and honoring God and your future husband with your body.

 Flee from sexual immorality. All other sins a [woman] commits are outside [her] body, but [she] who sins sexually sins against [her] own body. Do you not know that your body is a temple of the Holy Spirit, who is in you, whom you have received from God? You are not your own; you were bought at a price. Therefore honor God with your body.

1 Corinthians 6:18-20

"but we're in love!"

> Love is as strong as death, its jealousy unyielding as the grave. It burns like blazing fire, like a mighty flame.
>
> SONG OF SONGS 8:6

Earlier it was pointed out that fire has both benefits and dangers, but consider this question: What is the difference between a safe fire in a fireplace and a raging fire on a mountainside? One has firm boundaries, the other has no boundaries at all. The same thing is true in your relationship with your boyfriend. If you have firm boundaries and refuse to let anyone cross them, your dating life can be romantic and enjoyable. But without firm boundaries, your dating relationships can quickly become dangerous and destructive as you find yourself going much further than you ever intended.[1] Andrea, Leslie, and Cori learned this firsthand.

LESSONS LEARNED THE HARD WAY

Andrea can testify that if you don't establish healthy boundaries early in a dating relationship, you could send your boyfriend the wrong message and find yourself in a place you don't want to be.

> Because of the way I flirted with my boyfriend during our relationship, I aroused him sexually, and our relationship consisted of long make-out sessions. The more I did it, the easier it was to justify. I figured everyone does stuff like this and that he must really love and care for me to want to make out with me so much.
>
> One day we were playing Ping Pong and the ball bounced into a dark storage room. When we both went to get it, he closed the door, took off his pants, and started fumbling with mine. I wondered what would make him

think I'd have sex with him, especially in a storage room! I backed away and told him this was a direction I was not ready to take.

Leslie says that she had planned on being a virgin when she marries, and her father gave her a purity ring as a symbol of that commitment. However, that dream faded into a memory once she and her boyfriend began having sex. Leslie says:

> Although we were both committed to purity, once we began French kissing, my emotions and hormones went flying! We'd have sex, feel bad about it, ask God's forgiveness, stay pure for a week, and then fall into the same sin again. Eventually we broke up when I moved away to do an internship, but the secrecy of my sin still festered in my heart. I sat there during my quiet times, staring into space, unable to hear from the Lord at all.
>
> I knew I had to make things right and confess my sin. Sobbing, I called my dad to tell him that I was going to send back my purity ring because I had failed to keep my promise. He blew me away when he responded, "Leslie, you keep that ring on your finger, because I'm giving you a second chance and I trust that you will follow through this time." I know God was using my dad to show me His love. Coming clean with my parents is one of the hardest things I've ever done, but I knew it was necessary for me to ever feel fully restored. From here on out, I'm not going to arouse a guy to go further than I want to go or do anything I wouldn't want my parents or God to know about.

We admire Leslie's courage in confessing to her parents and her determination to learn from her mistakes and move on with better boundaries. Way to be, Leslie! You go, girl!

As Leslie and her boyfriend discovered, sexual passion can escalate quickly. If you don't have firm boundaries in your relationship with your boyfriend, know that it's never too late to back up and establish some. Don't let guilt keep you in an unsafe place. Simply learn from your mistakes and maintain better boundaries in the future.

Cori's confusion about the line between safe and unsafe physical activities led her to do things that she also regrets, but she's not going to let that stop her from establishing better boundaries in future relationships, either. She says this:

> I started reading *Every Young Man's Battle* and it was like, "Wow!" The key
> phrase that has stuck with me is, *Clearly, caressing the breast is [sexual] foreplay.*
> Man, did that hit me like a speeding bullet. I had let my boyfriend do that
> and really didn't think anything of it. Later, when I was going out with a dif-
> ferent guy, I went that far and even farther. I allowed him to touch not just
> my breasts, but my genital area as well, which is something I swore I'd never
> do. I have kicked myself so hard for letting that happen. I finished your
> whole book last night and have a new understanding about guys and about
> my need for better boundaries in my relationships. Now if a guy says, "I can't
> help the way I am! I can't control it!" I can say, "Yes, you *can* control it!" I'm
> going to control myself too. I'm not going to engage in "foreplay" anymore.

If you've gone too far, whether you did so intentionally or accidentally, you can have a fresh start as well. Don't focus on your past failures. God is merciful and wants to draw you back into a love relationship with Him no matter how far down the wrong path you've traveled. Ask Him to forgive you and to guide you down a better path. Jesus Christ died to give you a clean slate—your free gift for the tak-ing. Simply focus on your future success as you experience the Holy Spirit giving you the strength to live a life of sexual integrity.

THIS IS THE TIME TO ESTABLISH TRUST

Every time you choose to passionately kiss or touch a guy in a sexual way, you are sending a message that he can treat you like his little plaything. Every time you hold on to your boundaries, you teach him that you are a young woman of integrity who is worth the wait. If he is too impatient to wait until marriage, then *he's* risky mar-riage material anyway. If you are too impatient to wait until marriage, you are learn-ing patterns that make you risky marriage material too. You want to be able to trust each other wholeheartedly, and dating is a season in which you earn that trust. He will either prove himself to be a young man of integrity and a good candidate for a lifelong, committed marriage, or he will prove himself to be a selfish man of compromise who probably couldn't control his sexual passions even with a wedding band on his finger.

You will also prove yourself to be one or the other. Which will you choose?

HOW FAR CAN WE GO IF WE'RE "GOING OUT"?

If you have a boyfriend, you'll probably want to know the answer to one of the most common questions we get from couples who are dating—"How far *can* we go?" Of course, no one says you *have* to go any further physically with a boyfriend than you would with a male friend. You can have a great relationship that simply involves talking, getting to know each other, spending time with each other's family, going fun places and doing cool things together, and enjoying life as boyfriend and girlfriend.

> "It may not be cool or popular for me to say that I want to save sex until marriage in a world where virginity is considered little more than a hot potato that many want to get rid of. But I am saying it anyway, because I know there are a lot of guys out there who want the same thing."
>
> —WADE

In order to determine what safe, healthy boundaries look like for dating relationships, let's pick up where we left off in the last chapter. When a couple moves from being "friends" to "going out" as an exclusive couple, it's important that they set a slow pace for the physical aspect of their relationship so that they don't blindly gallop into sexually tempting situations. Of course, we are assuming that the couple has been friends long enough to truly know each other's character (we recommend at least one year) and that their parents support the relationship. We also assume you understand by this point in the book that it's not acceptable to touch any private body parts in a premarital relationship, whether it involves oral sex, anal sex, vaginal sex, mutual masturbation, bumping and grinding with clothes on, breast stimulation, or any other erotic activities that you wouldn't normally do if your parents were watching. It may sound like a strange boundary to imagine, but it works!

But let's talk more about the different stages of physical intimacy in romantic relationships, so that you can establish some wise boundaries that will help you guard your body in the battle for sexual integrity. Wise boundaries will also give you the confidence and freedom to enjoy this special relationship without fear of extreme temptations or sexual compromise.

HAND-IN-HAND (OR ARM-IN-ARM) INTIMACY

This level of physical intimacy involves holding hands or walking arm in arm. When you walk hand in hand or arm in arm with a guy, it's a sure sign you are more than friends. Both actions symbolize that you are choosing to travel together through this season of life and that you are not ashamed of your feelings for each other.

At this level of intimacy, he's probably walking you around campus, books tucked under one arm with the other arm around your waist or holding your hand, or perhaps he's opening doors for you and escorting you in with his hand gently in the middle of your back. Again, this is acceptable, provided you feel comfortable with this level of intimacy.

FACE-TO-FACE INTIMACY

The closer and more comfortable you feel with someone, the more naturally you'll want to be in each other's space. This closer-than-usual stance most often takes the form of face-to-face intimacy. Whereas you stood maybe three or four feet away from one another as acquaintances or friends, as a couple you may naturally stand closer to one another and have more face-to-face time.

At this level of intimacy, it's a good idea to talk with your boyfriend about your preference regarding kissing before marriage. Some of your peers are committing to save their kisses for their future spouse and don't want someone "stealing" their first or any other kiss. If that's how you feel, give him fair warning so he doesn't cross this boundary. Or ask him if this is how he feels so you don't rob him of this precious gift, either.

If neither of you has a conviction about saving your kisses until marriage, we recommend that you avoid kissing for extended lengths of time (more than three seconds). We also recommend that you avoid "tongue to tongue" intimacy (French kissing) altogether. Deep, passionate kissing is a surefire way to get your sexual juices flowing! Also be aware that some sexually transmitted diseases, such as herpes, can be transmitted by mouth-to-mouth contact or saliva exchange, another reason to guard not just your body, but also your mouth for marriage someday.

LISTEN TO YOUR RADAR

If at any point you sense a radar alarm going off in your spirit that says, *WARNING! This doesn't feel right!* listen to it. Don't ignore your mind or your heart telling you to slow down. Let your conscience be your guide. God put that radar there. You may have ignored it in the past, but you can learn to listen for it again. If things get a little too close to compromise, let that radar guide you and resist doing things that make you uncomfortable or that you feel may be wrong. If you ignore those warnings, you may become desensitized to them when they are alerting you to real danger. But if you submit to your radar and let it be your guide, it will keep you safe.

When that radar begins to get your attention, simply smile and say to your boyfriend, "I'd prefer you not do that, okay?" You don't have to be offensive, just invite him to support your boundaries. If he continues to push your boundaries, trying to get you to do things you don't feel comfortable doing, get offensive if necessary. Let him know that if he can't respect you, he can't spend time with you. Remember, no one else can guard your body and your sexual purity. That's your job.

IT'S WORTH THE WAIT

How long do you intend to live? A long time? Let's say you plan to live until you are ninety. Imagine your life of ninety years as a timeline, similar to the ones you learned about in math class. Yours might look like this:

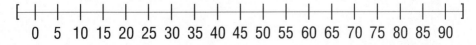

Now put an *X* on the number that represents your current age. Then put an *X* on the number that represents the age you would like to be by the time you get married. Now step back and look at the big picture of this timeline. Even though it may seem like forever before God allows you to enjoy a sexual relationship, how long is it compared to the rest of your life? When you can enter into marriage without emotional baggage, sexually transmitted diseases, unplanned pregnancies, and other symptoms of compromise, you will enhance your ability to enjoy sex with your husband for many, many years to come.

To give you an image of just how worth the wait sex really is, we'd like to share a passage from *The Mystery of Marriage* by Mike Mason:

> What moment in a man's life can compare with that of the wedding night, when a beautiful woman takes off all her clothes and lies next to him in bed, and that woman is his wife? What can equal the surprise of finding out that the one thing above all others which mankind has been most [creative] in dragging through the dirt turns out in fact to be the most innocent thing in the world? Is there any other activity at all which an adult man and woman may engage in together (apart from worship) that is actually more childlike, more clean and pure, more natural and wholesome and unequivocally right than is the act of making love? For if worship is the deepest available form of communion with God…then surely sex is the deepest communion that is possible between human beings.[2]

Yes, God intends for your sex life to be absolutely fantastic and to be something that bonds you and your husband together like superglue. By establishing and maintaining healthy physical boundaries in your premarital relationships, you'll be free to enjoy the wonder of sex on your honeymoon night—and the rest of your life—without regrets.

 Marriage should be honored by all, and the marriage bed kept pure.

Hebrews 13:4

looking for love in the right places

when the time is right
for mr. right

Many waters cannot quench love; rivers cannot wash it away.

SONG OF SONGS 8:7

Love. More songs, plays, movies, and books have been written about it than any other theme in history. It's more intoxicating than the most fragrant rose, the finest of wine, or the richest of foods. No words can fully describe how incredibly marvelous and magical love can be. Nor can words fully describe how potentially painful love can be, and that's why it's so important that you not rush into love. This book wouldn't be complete if we didn't answer these questions about love:

- When is the right time for love?
- How do I know if he's Mr. Right?
- How do I know if it's really love?
- How can I protect love once I find it?

WHEN IS THE RIGHT TIME FOR LOVE?

Every woman has her own unique timeline when it comes to finding Mr. Right, but most go through four seasons:

1. The Exploration Season
2. The Consideration Season
3. The Commitment Season
4. The Cementing Season

The Exploration Season begins when you first start feeling attracted to guys, usually somewhere between age ten and sixteen, and lasts until you are ready to consider entering into a committed relationship if the right guy were to come along. During this fun time you are getting to know different young men as friends in order to discover what you would like and dislike in a potential mate.

For instance, you notice that Ben drives you crazy with his overly serious attitude, but Scottie makes you and your friends laugh hysterically because he is just *so funny*, and you realize that you'd like Mr. Right to have a good sense of humor. Or perhaps you've noticed how Jared seems to have a different girlfriend every other week, and you decide that you want to be with a guy who demonstrates the desire and ability for long-term commitment and faithfulness. You get the idea.

Use this time to explore other people's personalities and character traits so you can form your own opinions about what kind of person you would like to wake up to every morning. The length of this season varies from person to person. It can begin as early as elementary school with the first boy you find yourself attracted to, and it can extend well into adulthood as you continue contemplating relationships with interesting guy friends until you know what kind of guy you would like to have as a husband. But when you are finally ready to consider a serious relationship with the right guy, should he come along, your season begins to change.

During the Consideration Season you consciously begin the search for Mr. Right because you know what you are looking for in a mate and feel you are ready to find a lifetime marriage partner. Through the process of elimination, you will rule out certain young men who don't meet your criteria, for whatever reason. During this season you will probably go out on individual or group dates to continue getting to know a young man who you think has potential for a serious relationship: He has no major character flaws, appears to fit your mold, and is acceptable to your friends and family. You spend time getting to know him in person, over the phone, and through letters and e-mails. All the while you are asking yourself, "Could *this* be Mr. Right?"

When you've gotten to know a young man well enough to appreciate him as a friend and love him as a boyfriend, and you have decided that he is a good match for you, you enter the next season.

In the Commitment Season emotions are elevated, hopes are heightened, and dreams for your marriage and possibly a future family swirl in your mind. Oh sure, you've probably been dreaming of marriage and motherhood before this time, but up until this point, your potential groom has had a blank face in these healthy fantasies. Now, the face in the wedding fantasy is in focus, and you rejoice that you've solved the mystery of Mr. Right's true identity.

The Cementing Season is the season of your marriage. You have vowed to leave your mother and father and cleave only to your husband for the rest of your life.

You promise to love him in sickness and in health, for richer or poorer, through good times and bad. You shamelessly offer your body and become one flesh with your Mr. Right.

Before we move on to the next question, here's a word of caution: Extremely long-term dating relationships can increase sexual temptation, and we don't recommend them. That's why we keep saying that time is your friend—don't rush into a committed relationship. Keep in mind that if you gallop through the exploration and consideration seasons when you are thirteen or fourteen, you will have at least five years or so before you will be able to make a lifelong commitment to someone. That's a really long time to be with one person and continue to guard your mind, heart, and body against sexual compromise. That's why we recommend that you wait at least until your senior year of high school before you commit to a guy as boyfriend and girlfriend. Then if you discern that you've found Mr. Right, waiting a year or two won't be as difficult as having to wait four or five. Use the time to get to know yourself and what qualities you want in a future husband. You'll be much more likely to choose someone who is a good match for you.

How Do I Know If He's Mr. Right?

Does God have only one guy for you? Can only one man be your soul mate? Of course not. God does not cruelly hide Mr. Right somewhere on the planet, and then say, "Okay, now you have to find him!" Many young men could qualify as your Mr. Right, but you get to choose which one you want to commit to. However, even if you do not choose wisely and marry Mr. Wrong, when you recite your wedding vows, he automatically becomes your Mr. Right. It's God's will that you be a committed wife to this man, through good times and bad, regardless of the character flaws that may surface down the road. If you're wise you'll enjoy the exploration season for many years so that you can truly discern the best match for you.

What does a good potential mate look like? While some would say "tall, dark, and handsome," we recommend that you consider these five things:

1. *Spiritual maturity and Christlike character.* Does he love God? attend church? worship and share his faith unashamedly? serve others in helpful ways, especially his immediate family? Does he exhibit the fruits of the

Holy Spirit—love, joy, peace, patience, kindness, goodness, gentleness, faithfulness, and self-control? If he's going to be the spiritual leader of your household someday, spiritual maturity should be on the top of your wish list.

2. *Strong family background* (or at least the desire to develop one). Remember, you don't just marry him, you marry his whole family. While you may not enjoy spending time with his parents and siblings quite as much as with him, you'll spend many future holidays and family vacations with these people.

   While it would be ideal if he comes from a home where both parents are committed and healthy Christians, a person from a broken home or from a non-Christian home can also make a good mate. However, if you know he comes from a dysfunctional family, and all of our families are somewhat dysfunctional, invest extra time in getting to know him to see if he understands how to have a healthy relationship. Make sure he's committed to being the best husband and father he can be, regardless of the examples he may have had. (By the way, if you come from a broken home or dysfunctional family, you may choose poorly when it comes to romantic relationships unless you seek healing from your own personal childhood wounds. Spend extra time developing good, close friendships with both guys and girls and learn to relate in healthy ways before committing to a serious relationship.)

3. *Financial responsibility.* If he's going to be the financial provider for you and your children someday, he needs to know how to make money, budget that money, and save money. If he doesn't have a savings account or a dime to his name, he may be Mr. Not Right Now. Be sure he gets his financial ducks in a row before you commit to him.

4. *Vision for the future.* Look for someone who has a general idea of God's plan for his life, knows what he wants to do and where he wants to go, and has a logical plan for how to get there. Also be sure his vision is compatible with your own. If you become his wife, you will pledge to be his helpmate and to go wherever God guides him. Although your interests

can vary greatly, in general they need to flow in the same direction. Don't be one of the many people who marry so early in life that they don't know what they want their future to look like. By the time they figure it out, it's often contrary to what their spouse wants to do. When this happens, one of them must sacrifice his or her own dreams or they grow apart as they grow old.

5. *Physical attractiveness.* Notice that this falls at the bottom of our list, but it is on the list nonetheless. While it's completely unimportant that your Mr. Right look like some jock or celebrity, it is vital that he appeals to you physically. Even if he loves God, has strong family relationships, is great with money, and has a promising future, if you don't find him physically attractive, *don't marry him.* That may sound cold, but you will not want to give your body frequently to a man you don't find physically attractive, and it is neither wise nor loving to marry him if you feel this way. In fact, it's downright cruel. Wouldn't you be devastated if you discovered your husband wasn't physically attracted to you at all? A guy will feel the same way.

HOW DO I KNOW IF IT'S REALLY LOVE?

This question reflects the wrong belief that love is a feeling. Most married couples will tell you that some days they "feel" like they are in love and other days they don't feel like it at all. Feelings are fickle, but love is not a feeling. Love is a commitment. So if you want to know if you really love a particular guy, ask yourself, "Am I really committed to this person?" If not or if your commitment is conditional, then you don't love him. If you are committed to loving that person unconditionally, even on the days that you find it difficult, then yes, it's love.

Paul wrote about true love in 1 Corinthians 13:4-8:

Love is patient, love is kind. It does not envy, it does not boast, it is not proud. It is not rude, it is not self-seeking, it is not easily angered, it keeps no record of wrongs. Love does not delight in evil but rejoices with the truth. It always protects, always trusts, always hopes, always perseveres. Love never fails.

Rest assured that a guy loves you if his love passes the test of time, and he consistently treats you with dignity, respects your boundaries, protects you, trusts you, and always wants the best for you. But if he doesn't do these things, he doesn't love you unconditionally—and you shouldn't marry him. Also see if your love passes the test of time and has the same characteristics.

How Can I Protect Love?

Once you've found a potential Mr. Right and have entered the commitment season, you can do three things to enhance romance instead of ruining it:

1. *Respect the fact that he has a life apart from you.* Don't smother him—he's your boyfriend, not your Siamese twin. Don't expect him to spend all of his free time catering to your emotional needs. Encourage him to pursue his own hobbies and spend time with his other close friends, and you do the same. Don't intentionally distract him from things that are vitally important to him right now, such as making good grades or working to earn extra money. Your patience will pay off in the long run as he appreciates the fact that you are supportive of him, his relationships, and his personal goals. Then when he comes around to spend time with you, you'll know it's because he *wants* to, not because he feels like he *has* to.

2. *Let him lead.* One of the fastest ways you can get a guy to stop pursuing you is by rushing him into a commitment that he's not ready to make. If he's not ready to commit to marriage, he may simply need more time. Respect the fact that he's not ready and be patient, or move on to explore the possibility that there's a different Mr. Right out there for you. You really don't want any guy making a premature, halfhearted commitment to you. If he says he's not ready, he may be doing you a big favor and saving you a lot of heartache in the long run. If you are patient until he's ready, then when he says, "I do," you'll know that he really does.

3. *Practice delayed gratification by not living together, and resist any type of sexual involvement.* In a *Christianity Today* poll, 70 percent of teens overall and 50 percent of Christian teens said they thought living together prior to marriage (cohabitating) was perfectly acceptable.[1] Many young women attempt to secure their relationship with a guy by becoming sexual with him, thinking that if she gives him her body, he'll never leave. *Don't be fooled.* Remember, what a guy usually wants most is sex, and if he's already getting sex, why should he give up his freedom and get married? Like Mama used to say, "Why will he buy the cow if he already gets the milk for free?" Good things come to those who wait, and a sexual relationship is well worth the wait. Delaying sexual gratification now can set your marriage up for a lifetime of sexual gratification later.

DON'T MISS THE ULTIMATE MR. RIGHT

In closing this discussion, don't forget there's a Mr. Right who longs for your attention and affection, who stands ready to engage in a more passionate love relationship than you could ever imagine. He's already made enormous sacrifices to demonstrate His unconditional love for you. He comes from the strongest family you could imagine, and His Father set an example of perfect love for Him to follow. He owns everything in both heaven and earth and can provide for you beyond your wildest dreams. He has a great vision for your future together, which includes a never-ending honeymoon together in paradise.

While you are single, won't you take advantage of every possible opportunity to bask in the incomparable love of Jesus Christ?

And I pray that you, being rooted and established in love, may have power, together with all the saints, to grasp how wide and long and high and deep is the love of Christ, and to know this love that surpasses knowledge—that you may be filled to the measure of all the fullness of God.

Ephesians 3:17-19

becoming mrs. right

> The LORD God said, "It is not good for the man to be alone. I will make
> a helper suitable for him."
>
> GENESIS 2:18

If you happened to walk into a room where six handsome, Christian young men were talking about what they are looking for in a wife someday, would you want to be a fly on the wall? Would you want to listen in on their uncensored conversation? Sure! Well, that's how this chapter came about.

We asked six young men, "What are the top ten characteristics you will be looking for in Mrs. Right?" Their answers are listed, along with our instructions on how to develop these qualities in your life. The list isn't presented in any particular order, except everyone agreed that they considered the first one to be by far the most important. Although other qualities were discussed, all agreed with each of the following criteria.

1. SHE HAS A PERSONAL RELATIONSHIP WITH JESUS CHRIST

Are you involved in church or a youth group? Are you working on becoming a better disciple of Christ and looking for ways to serve Him? Are you reading God's Word and praying for a deeper revelation of who God is? When you pursue God like crazy, you'll be amazed at how He molds you into someone other people are drawn to and want to get to know. If a guy is initially drawn to your Christlike character, he likely also loves God.

2. She Takes Care of Herself
and Has a Positive Self-Image

What did they mean when they said they were looking for a young woman who "takes care of herself"? They want a woman whose weight is relatively proportionate to her height; who has clean skin, well-kept hair and nails; and who takes pride in how she dresses and looks in public.

Let's face it, guys are visually stimulated. While some of the guys tried to say this in just the right way, none of them could deny that they want a girl who is relatively attractive. One said, "She doesn't have to be a beauty queen or a cover model, just nice looking." Another added, "Her inner beauty is more of what will make her beautiful to me than what's on the outside." Some complained that they had dated stereotypically "beautiful" women in the past but found that over time they became unattractive because of their personalities. Others became less beautiful because they were insecure and needed to be complimented and affirmed constantly. The guys also said they don't like it when their girlfriends feel the need to "fish" for compliments. They want a young woman whose confidence comes from within, not from them.

3. She Is Generally a Happy Person
and Has a Positive Outlook on Life

No one likes being with a sourpuss, a whiner, or a complainer. By nature, we are drawn to happy people who lift others up. Don't make the mistake of thinking, *Well, if I could just find Mr. Right, I would be a happy person!* Psychologists studied fifteen years' worth of data on twenty-four thousand people and found, "Being married boosts happiness only one-tenth of a point on an eleven-point scale.... Most people are no more satisfied with life after marriage than they were before.... Although happiness rises after exchanging vows, most people return to their pre-marriage level within two years."[1] Marriage is not the answer to anyone's misery.

Don't take yourself—or life—too seriously. Learn to look at the bright side of things. There's usually a silver lining behind every dark cloud. Laugh often, especially at yourself. If depression darkens your life for more than two straight months, talk with your parents, pastor, or doctor about possible causes and whether you need professional help.

4. SHE EXERCISES SELF-CONTROL AROUND OTHER GUYS

You may be surprised to hear this, but most guys admit to being relatively jealous creatures. When they like a girl, they don't want to see her acting overly friendly with other guys. One young man said, "If I'm in a serious relationship with someone, I want to know that I'm the only one for her. I don't want to see her getting all giddy around another guy and then have to worry that she's about to dump me for him." While these guys made clear that they expected their girlfriends to have other male friends, they also expected to share in these friendships once they started dating exclusively.

5. SHE IS CAREFUL WITH MONEY AND CAN BUDGET WISELY

Many young men worry about what kind of providers they'll be for their families. They realize that the burden of responsibility to put food on the table and pay the bills will likely rest on their shoulders. One young man said, "If I'm going to work hard to earn the money, I want my wife to work hard to stretch it as far as possible."

One way to ensure that you will be careful with money and budget wisely when you marry is to begin doing so now, with whatever money or income you have. This includes not expecting your parents to hand you anything you want on a silver platter. If you do, you may put pressure on your husband to do the same. Be responsible about what you purchase, and if you have a credit card, don't ever spend more money than you can pay off each month. Don't make the mistake of going into credit-card debt and paying interest payments. You don't want to walk into marriage someday as a financial burden because you are in debt. Practice being careful with money now and walk into your marriage someday as an asset, not a liability.

6. She Has Good Relationships with Her Family and Has Close Friendships

Do you want to know what the best practice for marriage is? Living in a family. If you can't live in relative peace with your family and don't have any close friendships, it could be because you are hard to get along with—and a healthy guy will see this as a red flag. Although you and your parents may have typical mother-daughter or father-daughter squabbles, are there times when you can enjoy one another's company and do things together without arguing? Can you admit when you are wrong and ask forgiveness? Can you forgive others and choose to love them in spite of their shortcomings? Do people enjoy being friends with you because you know how to give-and-take in a relationship? Practicing these things now is great preparation for becoming Mrs. Right.

7. She Is Nurturing and Would Make a Good Mother Someday

Guys want their kids to have enjoyable childhood experiences, and they want a wife who will nurture their children and take pride in being a good mom. Of course, most guys look forward to being the best daddy they can be and plan on helping out with the parenting. But children require an enormous amount of time and energy and so, by God's perfect design, both mom and dad need to provide for their child's many physical, emotional, mental, and spiritual needs. You may be very career-minded, but if you plan to have a family, you may have to be willing to sacrifice or postpone some personal goals for the sake of raising emotionally healthy children.

Before my husband and I had our first child, I was a premed student. However, on my daughter's first birthday, I cried because I felt as if I had missed so much of that special first year because of all the time I'd spent in classes and studying. I knew it would only get more intense as I entered medical school, so I made one of the hardest decisions I've ever made. I finished my bachelor's degree but gave up on the idea of going to medical school for the sake of my family. It's a decision I've never regretted, and although I have worked part-time outside the home as a youth minister and speaker, the additional time and deep bond I enjoy with my children is far more rewarding than any medical career I could have had.

8. She Is Supportive of What I Want to Do with My Life and Encourages Me

More than anything, a husband needs his wife to be his cheerleader. Mr. Right will want you to be his biggest fan. It's inevitable that you will go through some hard times. You may face great losses, such as the loss of a job, the death of loved ones, or even the loss of a child. He may want to change careers, which could create some enormous financial challenges. As a man wades through the decisions and disappointments that life presents, he needs a partner who will be in his corner, a woman who stands by her man.

I know a woman who married a lawyer, partly because she thought she'd never have to worry about finances because of his career. However, by the time her husband was forty, he was burned out and didn't want to practice law anymore. He decided he wanted to be a high school teacher, even though it meant a huge cut in his salary. But his wife couldn't accept this drastic lifestyle change, and after many years of tension and bitterness, they divorced. Her love for him was conditional, based on his paycheck. When you consider whether a young man is Mr. Right, ask yourself: "Am I this man's biggest fan? Do I respect him and trust him enough to be his cheerleader?" Make sure you are committed to supporting and encouraging him every step of the way down life's road.

9. She Has Her Own Dreams and Goals That I Can Help Her Fulfill

Do you know what your passions are in life? What do you like to do? What kind of things energize and motivate you? A college education can be a great way to discover the kinds of things that stimulate, energize, or inspire you. When I was in college I remember thinking, *How lame that I have to earn a P.E. credit!* I took a scuba diving class and discovered a love for underwater life I never knew I had. I also remember thinking, *Enough English courses already! Why do I have to take English every single year of high school?* But you know what? It helped me be a much better writer and communicator, and that is my passion in life. A childhood development class helped me understand my children better and be a better mom, which has always been and will always be a goal of mine. If you develop your own interests and discover your own passions, you will be a more happy, interesting, well-rounded person.

10. SHE IS ADVENTUROUS AND CAN ENJOY AT LEAST SOME OF MY HOBBIES

Guys are typically adventurous creatures, and they want a woman who can share some of those adventures with them. How adventurous are you? If you don't have any interests or hobbies, you can begin developing some. For instance, attend cultural arts festivals or take trips to local museums or take a class to learn an unusual skill such as woodworking or interior design. Join the drama or debate team. Check into classes offered at a local junior college to learn how to speak a foreign language, sculpt, design Web sites, or something else that floats your boat. Do something that gets you out of your comfort zone and teaches you new ways to have fun.

Of course, each person has his or her own ideas of what adventure looks like. When my husband and I first dated, my idea of fun was shopping, but Greg's was playing softball. So that we could both do things we enjoyed, we often spent Friday evening after work shopping, and on Saturday I'd sit in the bleachers cheering on my handsome first baseman. Many times I was tempted to say, "I'll spend Saturday shopping while you play softball, and we'll get together that evening," but that wouldn't have been nearly as fun as when we spent time together.

Regardless of what your Mr. Right's passions may be, find some that are fun for the both of you and enjoy them together. Life is too short not to have fun, and having fun together strengthens any relationship.

BEING GOD'S MRS. RIGHT

Although you may be nowhere near ready to be any guy's Mrs. Right, you can be God's Mrs. Right in this season of singleness and every year that you are living and breathing. Perhaps you've never really considered God as someone who needs a wife, but guess what anyone who believes in Him and belongs to His church is called? The bride of Christ. Even though God can do anything without our help, He chooses to do things *through* us. His greatest desire for humans is for them to be His hands to reach out to those in need of His touch, His feet to go wherever He leads, and His mouthpiece to reveal His words and His will to others. He needs a helpmate, a Mrs. Right, to accomplish His goals and pursue His dreams with Him.

Partnering with God brings a far greater reward and sense of fulfillment than any other pursuit you could imagine. To find out more about what it takes to be *God's* Mrs. Right, read the next chapter.

"Let us rejoice and be glad and give him glory! For the wedding of the Lamb has come, and his bride has made herself ready. Fine linen, bright and clean, was given her to wear." (Fine linen stands for the righteous acts of the saints.)

Revelation 19:7-8

falling in love with Jesus

I am my beloved's and my beloved is mine.

Song of Solomon 6:3, NRSV

A radiant bride greeted her guests with a brilliant smile as she entered the reception hall after the wedding ceremony. She gracefully moved about the room, the train of her white gown flowing along the floor behind her, her veil cascading down her button-adorned back.

She conversed with each guest one by one, taking the time to mingle and soak up the compliments. "You look absolutely lovely." "Your dress is divine." "I've never seen a more beautiful bride." "What a stunning ceremony." The lavish praises rang on and on. The bride couldn't be more proud or more appreciative of the crowd's adoration. She could have listened to them swoon over her all evening. As a matter of fact, she did.

But where was the groom? All the attention focused on the bride and never once did she call anyone's attention to her husband. She didn't even notice his absence at her side. Scanning the room, I searched for him, wondering, *Where could he be?*

I finally found him, but not where I expected him to be. The groom stood alone over in the corner of the room with his head down. As he stared at his ring, twisting the gold band that his bride had just placed on his finger, tears trickled down his cheeks and onto his hands. That is when I noticed the nail scars. The groom was Jesus.

He waited, but the bride never once turned her face toward her groom. She never held His hand. She never introduced the guests to Him. She operated independently of Him.

I awoke with a sick feeling in my stomach, realizing that I'd been dreaming. "Lord, is this how I made you feel when I was looking for love in all the wrong places?" I wept at the thought of hurting Him so deeply.

Unfortunately, this dream illustrates exactly what is happening between God and millions of His people. He betroths Himself to us, we take His name, and then we go about our lives looking for love, attention, and affection from every source under the sun except from the Son of God, the Lover of our souls.

Oh, how Jesus longs for us to acknowledge Him, to introduce Him to our friends, to withdraw to be alone with Him, to cling to Him for our identity, to gaze longingly into His eyes, to love Him with all our heart and soul.

What about you? Do you have this kind of love relationship with Christ? Do you experience the incredible joy of intimacy with the One who loves you with a passion that is far deeper, far greater than anything you could find here on earth? We know from experience that you can.

How Do I Get There from Here?

Maybe you are wondering how you can experience this deeper, more gratifying level of intimacy with Jesus Christ. It would help to look where the spiritual journey begins and how our relationship with God evolves as we travel down the path of spiritual maturity. Life coach and international lecturer Jack Hill (www.royal-quest.com) explains that there are six progressive levels of relationship with God, as explained by the following metaphors in Scripture:

- potter/clay relationship
- shepherd/sheep relationship
- master/servant relationship
- friend/friend relationship
- father/daughter relationship
- groom/bride relationship[1]

I believe God gave us these metaphors to increase our understanding of His complex personality and to help us better comprehend the depth of His perfect love for us. These metaphors illustrate the maturing of our love relationship with God. Just as children develop physically until they reach adulthood, believers in Christ develop spiritually in stages as we walk down the road to spiritual maturity.

As we examine the dynamics of each of these stages, try to identify the level of intimacy you are currently experiencing in your walk with God.

POTTER/CLAY RELATIONSHIP

When we first come to Christ, our spiritual life has little shape or form. We submit ourselves to Jesus Christ as our Savior and ask God to begin shaping us into what He wants us to be. "We are the clay, you are the potter; we are all the work of your hand" (Isaiah 64:8; see also Jeremiah 18:4-6). As a piece of clay, we can allow the Potter to mold us, but we cannot express our love back to Him. When we comply and feel God using us, we feel good about ourselves. When we mess up or don't have a clear sense of purpose, we feel distant from God. We often withdraw because we believe He is angry with us due to our poor performance. Ephesians 2:10 says, "For we are God's workmanship, created in Christ Jesus to do good works, which God prepared in advance for us to do." This affirms that it is important for us to submit to God and allow Him to shape our lives into something that brings Him honor. However, He doesn't want our relationship to stop there. He wants it to become deeper and more intimate.

SHEPHERD/SHEEP RELATIONSHIP

It may not be flattering to be compared to a sheep, but this metaphor illustrates how well God takes care of His people, just as a shepherd carefully tends his flock. God spoke through the prophet Ezekiel:

> For this is what the Sovereign LORD says: I myself will search for my sheep
> and look after them. As a shepherd looks after his scattered flock when he
> is with them, so will I look after my sheep. I will rescue them from all the
> places where they were scattered…. They will lie down in good grazing land,
> and there they will feed in a rich pasture on the mountains of Israel. I myself
> will tend my sheep and have them lie down, declares the Sovereign LORD.
> (34:11-12,14-15; see also the parable of the good shepherd in John 10:1-18).

Although sheep know the shepherd's voice and will follow him, they have no idea what the heart of the shepherd feels for them. Sheep can't share the shepherd's dreams and hopes. They are merely concerned with their daily need for food and water. While it is important for us to follow and trust God as our Caretaker and Provider as a sheep follows a shepherd, God longs for us to have a more personal relationship with Him.

MASTER/SERVANT RELATIONSHIP

While sheep stay outside, servants at least live in the same household as the master and talk with him, as long as it is business. The servant enjoys a more intimate relationship. The parable of the talents (see Matthew 25:14-30) and the parable of the ten minas (see Luke 19:11-27) refer to this level of relationship. However, servants know little of what is happening with the master, other than what they are directly involved with. A servant's value is derived from how well she can complete the master's will. While it is important for us to serve God wholeheartedly and do His will, God still longs to have an even greater level of intimacy than this.

FRIEND/FRIEND RELATIONSHIP

A servant's relationship with her master rests on business and performance, while love and mutual concern form the basis of a friend's relationship with a friend. Jesus spoke about this deeper level of intimacy that He shared with His disciples when He said, "I no longer call you servants, because a servant does not know his master's [personal] business. Instead, I have called you friends, for everything that I learned from my Father I have made known to you" (John 15:15). Jesus is saying, "I value you not just because of how you serve me, but because you share my heart." A friend's value lies not so much in what she does, but in who she is as a personal confidant.

God wants to be our friend, and He wants us to be His friends. We can experience this friendship level of intimacy. As James 2:23 tells us, "And the scripture was fulfilled that says, 'Abraham believed God, and it was credited to him as righteousness,' and he was called God's friend." Also, Proverbs 22:11 says, "[She] who loves a pure heart and whose speech is gracious will have the king for [her] friend."

Yet even as close as two friends can be, blood runs thicker than water.

FATHER/DAUGHTER RELATIONSHIP

As we realize and accept the truth that we are not just God's lump of clay, sheep, servant, or even friend, but also God's very own child, we can experience tremendous healing from childhood wounds and disappointments. We can allow God to be the Father or the Mother (He possesses the good qualities of both genders) that we so needed or wanted. We can be free from the burden of trying to perform or produce for Him when we understand that He loves us not for what we do but because we are His daughters. As wonderful and healing as a father/daughter relationship is, the groom/bride relationship promises the most intimate connection of all.

GROOM/BRIDE RELATIONSHIP

Once a woman becomes a bride, the focus of her life and priorities change, and all other people and priorities pale in comparison to her primary love relationship. Again, this metaphor illustrates a much deeper truth—God desires for us to love Him passionately, to find it delightful to simply be in His presence, and to know Him personally both publicly and privately. He longs for our focus and priorities to become aligned with His.

Perhaps you can imagine relating to God as Father, Savior, or Lord but are struggling with the idea of relating to God like you would a husband. While some may even say that it's irreverent to relate to God in such an intimate way, God has always longed for this kind of relationship with His chosen people. He said through the prophet Hosea, "I will betroth you to me forever; I will betroth you in righteousness and justice, in love and compassion. I will betroth you in faithfulness, and you will acknowledge the LORD" (2:19-20).

God extends to us an eternal commitment of love, a love so deep, so wide, and so great that we cannot possibly fully understand it. This gift should inspire us to reciprocate with as equal a gift of love as is humanly possible. What started out as an engagement relationship between God and His own in the Garden of Eden will come to fullness at the wedding supper of the Lamb when Jesus Christ returns to claim His bride, the church.

So how can you cultivate a bridal love for Jesus and enjoy this intimate relationship that He longs to have with you? By falling in love with Him and attempting to pursue Him as passionately as He has been pursuing us all along.

MAKING JESUS YOUR FIRST LOVE

If you have asked Jesus to live inside your heart, He wants to live there permanently, not just rent a room there during the seasons that you don't have a boyfriend. Don't force God to take a backseat to anyone. Keep guys in their rightful place in your heart, and make sure you keep Jesus as your first love. Of course God wants you to love other people, but not more than you love Him.

Consider these verses:

But seek first his kingdom and his righteousness, and all these things will be given to you as well. (Matthew 6:33)

Delight yourself in the LORD and he will give you the desires of your heart. (Psalm 37:4)

In other words, seek God first and foremost, and He'll bless you with the other desires of your heart. As you've read repeatedly throughout this book, a guy can only do so much to fill the emptiness in your heart. However, God can fill your heart to overflowing with the love and intimacy you crave.

If you are wondering how on earth that is possible, consider these questions: Have you ever felt as if you were in love? Remember how thoughts of him sent your heart and mind reeling with excitement? how he dominated your thoughts morning, noon, and night? how you could be available to talk to him at a moment's notice if you knew he was about to walk by? Remember how you would drop anything and everything when the phone rang, desperately hoping to hear his voice on the other line? Thoughts of the potential of this relationship consumed your world. No matter how hard you tried, you just couldn't get him off your mind, right? (Not that you tried all that hard!)

God longs for you to be that consumed with Him. Not that you can stay on a mountaintop like the one just described every day of your life (all love relationships go through peaks and valleys), but He desires to be your first love. He wants your thoughts to turn to Him throughout the good and the bad days. He wants you to watch expectantly for Him to work things out in your life and to sense Him inviting you into His presence. He aches for you to call out to Him and listen for His loving reply. Although He wants you to invest in healthy relationships with others, He wants you to be most concerned about your relationship with Him.

GIVING GOD EVERY CHANCE

Maybe you are thinking, *Oh, I've been hearing that all my life! The answer to all my problems is Jesus, Jesus, Jesus! I know Jesus, but I could never feel complete satisfaction with someone I can't even see or touch!* If that's the case, we can understand why you might challenge what we're saying. However, we can't help but wonder if you have truly pursued a satisfying relationship with God. We encourage you to honestly answer the following questions:

- Have I *really* invested much time in getting to know God personally and intimately?
- Do I read the Bible, searching for clues as to God's character and plan for my life?
- Have I given God as many chances as I have given young men? my fantasies? visits to chat rooms? and so on?
- Have I ever chosen to pray or dance to worship music or go for a walk with God instead of picking up the phone to call a guy when I'm lonely?
- Are there moments spent alone (masturbating, fantasizing, reading or looking at inappropriate materials, and so on) that I ignore God's presence in an attempt to satisfy myself?
- Do I believe that God can satisfy every single need I have?
- Am I willing to test this belief by letting go of all the things, people, thoughts, and so on that I use to medicate my pain, fear, or loneliness and by becoming totally dependent upon God?

God longs for you to test Him and try Him on this. Don't let doubt or guilt from past mistakes keep you from seeking this satisfying first-love relationship with Him. God does not despise you for the way you've tried to fill the void in your heart in the past. He longs to cleanse your heart and teach you how to guard it from future pain and loneliness.

> "Come now, let us reason together,"
> says the LORD.
> "Though your sins are like scarlet,
> they shall be as white as snow;
> though they are red as crimson,
> they shall be like wool." (Isaiah 1:18)

We know from experience that a deeply satisfying love relationship with Jesus Christ is very possible, and so do many young women we know. Consider the following comments:

Tara: I often sense Jesus inviting me to crawl into His lap, bury my face in His chest, and just cry my eyes out while He holds me. Not only do I know that my heavenly Father is always there for me and loves me unconditionally, I also know that He likes me, which is a great comfort.

Michelle: When I started spending consistent time with God—worshiping, praying, reading His word—I began to see who He really is, who I really am, and the love relationship He desires to have with me. The Bible has become a huge love letter especially to me from God. Scriptures seem to come alive and actually make sense to me now (something I never thought could happen). Now I can't wait to "run away" with Jesus and be alone with Him, and I do so every chance I get.

Diana: Even though I love the Lord, I've frequently gone through seasons where I felt very distanced from Him. During one of these dry spells, I went over to see a friend one night. When I walked into her room, she was worshiping God in the dark by candlelight, just dancing around the room with her arms in the air and singing along with a worship CD. Rather than interrupt her, I decided to join in. Unexpectedly, I felt as if God was sweeping me off my feet, smiling over me with His strong arms wrapped around me. I felt His presence more than I ever had before and I sensed Him say to me, "This is what it takes to stay in love." Now I am always trying to think up other ways that I can express my love for Him, knowing I'll feel His love in return.

SEEK HIM AND FIND HIM

Invest some time in getting to know your heavenly Bridegroom personally and intimately. Start by carving a few minutes out of each day to read His word. Hosea, Song of Songs, and the book of John are great places to start getting a glimpse of His immeasurable love. Take a walk alone just to talk with God and be sure to leave plenty of time to listen for what He may want to say to you. Although you won't hear Him with your physical ears, you can certainly experience Him with the eyes and ears of your heart. Look around at nature for clues of His love, such as the wildflowers He planted along the side of the road just for you, the birds that fly across the sky and demonstrate God's incredible creativity, and the ever-changing scenery of the cloud-dotted sky at sunset. When you notice these things, tell Him how much you appreciate Him and long to know Him better.

When you seek a more personal relationship with Him, you can't miss Him. Even if you have missed Him before, don't worry. He knows where to find you, and He *will* pursue you. As a matter of fact, He's pursuing you right now. The romantic intimacy Jesus offers you on a day-to-day, moment-by-moment basis is exactly what many women look for all their lives but never find in earthly relationships. After reading this book, you know that sex with some guy is not where you'll experience ultimate fulfillment. You will only find that by falling in love with Jesus, the One who made your mind, heart, and body and who knows exactly what you need to satisfy every part of it.

Basking in this love relationship with Jesus is the secret to winning the war against sexual temptations. He stands ready and able to help you guard your mind, heart, and body even in the midst of this sex-saturated world. Surrender your battle to God and ask Him to reveal His lavish love to you. And as you receive and rejoice over this deeper level of intimacy with Him, know that we rejoice with you.

> *Ask and it will be given to you; seek and you will find; knock and the door will be opened to you. For everyone who asks receives; he who seeks finds; and to [her] who knocks, the door will be opened.*
>
> *Matthew 7:7-8*

if you desire other women

As you have read through this book, you may have wondered, *How do these things apply to me if my feelings are for other girls instead of guys?* Let's start by examining where these desires come from, then look at what the Bible has to say about homosexuality, and finally provide some strategies for victory in this particular battle.

RECOGNIZING THE ROOT OF THE ISSUE

We believe that homosexual desires and tendencies are often rooted in dysfunctional family relationships. Perhaps you are drawn to other women because you have experienced a deep love and sense of security with your mother that you've never experienced with a father. Maybe Dad wasn't there for you or was too emotionally distanced to help you grow comfortable with the idea of receiving love, attention, and affection from a man. Or perhaps your father or another man sexually abused you, and so you have negative feelings toward men and feel you can't trust them.

Our culture may also contribute significantly to women's desires for one another. By the time this book comes out, Madonna and Britney Spears's bold display of passionate kissing on national television will be old news. We frequently see billboards throughout the country with two scantily clad women in a provocative pose. Several of the teen magazines we browsed through while researching material for this book pictured two brazen beauties in a very intimate embrace, often accompanied by an article about their lesbian relationship. Movies and even prime-time television often portray homosexuality as an acceptable alternative lifestyle. Many public schools are pushing for curriculum that includes family scenarios with "two mommies" or "two daddies."

Contrary to what some gay and lesbian rights activists and scientific researchers want us to think, we don't believe there is such a thing as "the gay gene" or that some people are "born gay." Unlike your sex or ethnicity, homosexuality isn't some predetermined condition that was passed onto you genetically when you were conceived in your mother's womb. A person develops these desires through a variety of different experiences, but you are not powerless to develop different, more healthy desires. As a matter of fact, hundreds of former gay and lesbian individuals have left their homosexual lifestyles and found wholeness in their newfound heterosexuality.[1]

WHAT DOES THE BIBLE SAY?

In case you have questioned how God feels about homosexual relations, simply read the first chapter of Romans in the New Testament. The apostle Paul makes it very clear that God does not condone sexually intimate relationships between people of the same sex.

However, we want you to know beyond a shadow of a doubt that although God hates the sin of homosexuality, just as He hates all sin, He passionately and unconditionally loves all sinners regardless of the sexual battles we face. Even if you struggle with desires for other women, God is absolutely crazy about you, and His life-transforming power is just as available to you as it is to anyone else who calls on His name for help in resisting sin.

MOVING IN THE RIGHT DIRECTION

First, don't assume that every strong emotional attachment you feel toward someone of the same sex is a homosexual desire. You may notice an attractive girl walking down the street, you may think your best friend is incredibly beautiful, or you may feel very drawn toward a female teacher, coach, or mentor. If so, it doesn't mean you are lesbian. God wired us to desire intimate relationships with other women, but we don't have to sexualize those desires. Enjoy close female friendships and make wonderful memories together. Feel free to give other girls a pat on the back or a hug or let them cry on your shoulder when they need to. But avoid talking with or touching one another in a sexual way, and distract yourself with other thoughts if you find that you are fantasizing about such things. Remember to guard not just your body, but your mind and heart as well.

If some relationships in your life cause you to stumble, you may have to make some difficult decisions to end such friendships altogether, especially if the person isn't respectful of your new boundaries. Remember that the Bible tells us to "*flee from sexual immorality*" (1 Corinthians 6:18, emphasis added). If this person is holding you back from growing spiritually and becoming the godly woman you were created to be, don't hesitate to flee altogether. There is no shame in running from sin, and God will certainly honor the sacrifices you make for the sake of righteousness.

If you can't seem to find the strength necessary to do this on your own and you need help to escape homosexual tendencies or desires, ask for it. Find a counselor skilled in helping people overcome this issue. Or contact Exodus International (www.exodus.to), an organization that helps thousands of Christians just like you with accountability in avoiding compromising behaviors and encouragement in pursuing healthier relationships. Don't let pride or embarrassment rob you of the hope and healing you deserve.

The choice is yours. When you have a personal relationship with Jesus Christ, you have His power available to you to help you resist any temptation and make whatever changes you need to make in order to pursue a lifestyle of sexual and emotional integrity. Also know that we are cheering you on and praying for you as you seek the healthy relationships God intends for you to enjoy.

Foreword

1. "Most Teens See Marriage and Kids in their Future," *Youthviews: the Newsletter of the Gallup Youth Survey,* June 2001, 2.

2. Pat Socia, *Weaving Character into Sex Education,* 1997 Project Reality, P.O. Box 97, Golf, IL, 60029-0097, www.projectreality.org/products/books.html.

3. National Campaign to Prevent Teen Pregnancy, *With One Voice, 2002: America's Adults and Teens Sound Off About Teen Pregnancy,* Annual Survey, quoted in SIECUS (Sexuality Information and Education Council of the United States), "Shop Talk," January 17, 2003, www.siecus.org/pubs/shop/volume7/shpv70052.html.

Chapter 2

1. This illustration comes from material presented at a conference put on by the Coalition for Abstinence Education, Colorado Springs, Colorado, October 1996.

Chapter 4

1. Gary R. Collins, *The Biblical Basis of Christian Counseling for People Helpers* (Colorado Springs: NavPress, 1993), 113.

Chapter 5

1. Meghan Bainum, quoted in Mary Beth Marklein, "Casual Sex, in Newsprint," *USA Today,* November 14, 2002, 9D.

Chapter 6

1. Sharon A. Hersh, *"Mom, I Feel Fat!"* (Colorado Springs: Shaw, 2001), 111.

Chapter 7

1. Corey Kilgannon, "Slain Girl Used Internet to Seek Sex, Police Say," *New York Times,* May 22, 2002, late edition, sec. B.
2. John Eldredge, *The Journey of Desire* (Nashville: Thomas Nelson, 2000), 74.

Chapter 8

1. Prevention & Motivation Programs, Inc., Sexual Abuse Facts and Statistics, P.O. Box 1960, 659 Henderson Drive, Suite H, Cartersville, GA, 30120, www.goodtouchbadtouch.com.
2. Emilie Buchwald, Pamela R. Fletcher, and Martha Roth, eds., *Transforming a Rape Culture* (Minneapolis: Milkweed, 1993), 9.
3. Robin Washaw, *I Never Called It Rape: The M.S. Report on Recognizing, Fighting, and Surviving Date Rape and Acquaintance Rape* (New York: HarperCollins, 1994).

Chapter 9

1. *Cosmopolitan* (November 2003), *CosmoGirl* (November 2003), *Twist* (October–November 2003).
2. *Teen People,* November 2003.
3. Alex Kuczynski, "Girls Gone Macho," *Orange County Register,* November 17, 2002.

Chapter 13

1. American Academy of Pediatrics, *Pediatrics* 95, no. 1, www.cfoc.org/EducatorRes/Facts/.
2. Ann Kearney-Cooke, quoted in Alex Kuczynski, "Girls Gone Macho," *Orange County Register,* November 17, 2002.

Chapter 14

1. *Teen People,* November 2003.
2. *Revolve: The Complete New Testament* (Nashville: Thomas Nelson, 2003).
3. "Woman in Love," *People,* November 12, 2001, 54.

4. "Woman in Love," 54.

5. Chuck Arnold, "Picks & Pans: Britney," *People*, November 12, 2001, 41.

Chapter 19

1. American Social Health Association, *Sexually Transmitted Diseases in America: How Many Cases and at What Cost?* (1998): 5.

2. The illustration of the female reproductive organs is provided by A.D.A.M. Used by permission.

3. Steve Bradshaw, "Vatican: Condoms Don't Stop AIDS," *Guardian Unlimited Special Report,* October 9, 2003, www.guardian.co.uk.

4. Medical Institute for Sexual Health (MISH), *HPV Press Release,* Austin, Texas (May 9, 2000).

5. Susan C. Weller, "A Meta-Analysis of Condom Effectiveness in Reducing Sexually Transmitted HIV," *University of Texas Medical Branch (UTMB) News,* June 7, 1993, *Social Science and Medicine,* 36:36:1635-44.

6. Ed Vitagliano, "Study Finds Teen Sex, Suicide Are Linked, *AFA Journal* October 2003, www.crosswalk.com/family/parenting/teens/1224668 .html.

7. Maggie Gallagher, "Failed Promises of Abortion," January 27, 2003, http://www.townhall.com/columnists/maggiegallagher/mg20030127 .shtml.

Chapter 20

1. *Seventeen,* "National survey conducted by *Seventeen* finds that more than half of teens ages 15–19 have engaged in oral sex," news release, February 28, 2000.

2. Walt Mueller, "Kids and Sex: New Rules!" *Youth Culture@Today,* newsletter of the Center for Parent/Youth Understanding (Fall 2003): 11.

3. Lisa Remez, "Oral Sex Among Adolescents: Is It Sex or Is It Abstinence?" *Family Planning Perspectives* 32, no. 6 (November–December 2000).

4. S. Edwards and C. Carne, "Oral Sex and the Transmission of Viral STIs," *Sexually Transmitted Infections* 74, no. 1 (1998):6-10.

5. Edwards and Carne, "Oral Sex," 74, no. 2, 95-100.

6. P. F. Horan, J. Phillips, and N. E. Hagan, "The Meaning of Abstinence for College Students," *Journal of HIV/AIDS Prevention & Education for Adolescents & Children* 1, no. 2 (1998):51-66.

Chapter 21

1. Youth Risk Behavior Surveillance System, National Center for Chronic Disease Prevention and Health Promotion, www.cdc.gov/nccdphp/dash/yrbs/pdf-factsheets/sex.pdf.
2. Mary Meehan, "Abstinence Pledges Not Very Effective," Knight Ridder, November 8, 2003, life section.
3. Natalie Krinsky, quoted in Mary Beth Marklein, "Casual Sex, in Newsprint," *USA Today*, November 14, 2002.
4. Anna Schleelein, quoted in Marklein, "Casual Sex."

Chapter 22

1. This illustration comes from material presented at a conference put on by the Coalition for Abstinence Education, Colorado Springs, Colorado, October 1996.
2. Mike Mason, *The Mystery of Marriage* (Portland: Multnomah, 1985), 121.
3. "Weekly Illustration Update," Sunday, August 10, 2003, www.preaching today.com.

Chapter 24

1. Carol Potera, "Get Real About Getting Married," *Shape,* September 2003, 36.

Chapter 25

1. Chart prepared by Jack Hill to encapsulate the points made in Craig W. Ellison, "From Eden to the Couch," *Christian Counseling Today* 10, no. 1 (2002): 30. Used with permission.

Afterword

1. Dr. James Dobson, *Focus on the Family* newsletter, June 2002, 4.

about the author

Shannon Ethridge is a wife, mother, writer, speaker, lay counselor, and missionary for sexual integrity. Speaking to youth, college students, and adult women since 1989, her passions include instilling sexual values in children at an early age, challenging young people to embrace a life of sexual purity, ministering to women who have looked for love in all the wrong places, and challenging all women to make Jesus Christ the primary Love of their life.

A regular instructor on the Teen Ministries Mania campus, Shannon has been featured numerous times on radio and television programs. She and her husband, Greg, have been married for fourteen years and live in a log cabin among the piney woods of east Texas with their two children, Erin (twelve) and Matthew (nine).

Shannon Ethridge Ministries

For speaking engagements or other resources available through Shannon Ethridge Ministries, go to www.shannonethridge.com or e-mail Shannon at SEthridge@shannonethridge.com.